KHAMSIN(

M000085861

THE POLITICIAN

AND OTHER STORIES

Third Edition

Translated by

DOMNERN GARDEN AND **HERBERT P. PHILLIPS**

Introduced by

HERBERT P. PHILLIPS

SILKWORM BOOKS

ISBN 974-7551-51-9

This edition first published by Silkworm Books in 2001

Silkworm Books
104/5 Chiang Mai–Hot Road, M. 7, T. Suthep, Muang,
Chiang Mai 50200, Thailand
E-mail address: silkworm@pobox.com
Website: http://www.silkwormbooks.com

Typeset by Silk Type in Garamond 11 pt.
Cover photograph © by Kanta Poonpipat
Printed in Thailand by O. S. Printing House, Bangkok

To my mother
who could not read

CONTENTS

INTRODUCTION

THE publication of this third edition of *The Politician and Other Stories* is meant to celebrate the seventieth birthday of the author, Khamsing Srinawk, also known by the nom de plume, Lao Khamhawm. This version includes translations of the twelve original short stories published prior to 1970 and translations of five additional stories, the most recent of which was written in 1995.

While a definitive history of twentieth-century Thai literature has yet to be written, there is little doubt that when it is published major attention will be given to the writings of Khamsing Srinawk. There are a number of reasons for this, both social-historical and literary. Perhaps the most fundamental is the exponential increase in literacy in Thailand during the twentieth century and in the kinds of literary materials and authors that have come to interest readers. Particularly after the 1932 revolution when Thailand changed from an absolute to a constitutional monarchy, literature expanded from a gossipy elite activity, often written by and for elite women (or middle-class women seeking elite models), into a literature authored principally by men, documenting the inequalities of Thai society and serving as a literature of social protest. Much of this literature was obviously a refraction of the dramatic social changes occurring in Thailand during the post-revolution and depression period of the 1930s. While Khamsing's writings two decades later were influenced by this international literary tradition, he clearly departed from it in emphasizing the individuality and down-to-earth humanity of his characters, particularly villagers, rather than portraying them as stereotyped victims of social oppression. His is a literature that memorializes the rich, subtle, ironic, and provocative features of his characters' total experience.

Thus, in a very real sense, Khamsing has over the past forty years created the concept of the Thai peasant as a literary hero. His heroes are hardly great men, but they are funny, imaginative, devious, and exceedingly thoughtful about their local worlds and their own ability to cope with, and sometimes even maximize, the circumstances of their lives. Through his storytelling talents Khamsing has transformed them into individuals with memorable literary identities. Admittedly, like virtually all other Thai writers, Khamsing does not address the inner lives of his characters or the kinds of complex indecision or turmoil found in the characterizations of contemporary Western fiction. Rather, the literary identities of Khamsing's actors are always a product of their relationships with others, and their relative success or failure in dealing with the opportunities of their cultural environment and their own limitations, including the cognitive confusions created by the incomprehensible changes occurring in virtually every area of Thai life.

Through his imagery Khamsing also directs his reader's attention to the power of some fundamental Thai verities, verities that in the chaos of the modern world are so easily forgotten. Thus, a few of his stories are about old men approaching the end of their current lives, inherently vulnerable, but managing to make do by earning the respect and trust of others for their limited capabilities. Old men do not easily transform into heroes, but because they are so much closer to the inescapable, but unknown, certainties of life, death, and the next world they can lead more ordinary, seemingly less vulnerable, people into foolish, self-defeating actions, as in the story *Intercourse*. Of a different order is the reference in *I Lost My Teeth* to the jungle as a place of refuge, not only from the incursions of criminals, but as a place where one can escape the demands of others, retain one's sanity, and pursue one's own interests. While these kinds of allusions are not unfamiliar to most Thai, their use in these stories as didactic memos is precisely what makes Khamsing's texts so memorable to Thai readers.

With the phenomenal growth of the Thai middle class in recent decades, Khamsing has also expanded his vision of the major participants in the Thai social world. Thus, the hero of *Paradise Preserved* is almost a prototypic expression of such a person who leaves behind his secure career as a school teacher to take maximum, if short-lived, advantage of the opportunities of Thailand's expanding economy, and how he deals in almost picaresque fashion with the unforeseen power of larger sociopolitical forces. His is essentially a cameo version of the Thai national experience during the last quarter of the twentieth century.

Khamsing's own life and career is much richer and more distinctive than that of the hero of *Paradise Preserved* but in its larger historical contours is not too radically different. Born in a village in Khorat Province, then five miles from the closest town, he read virtually anything he could get his hands on while tending his family's buffaloes. An uncle who was a monk encouraged him to read and study, and other family members supported his attending secondary school. He came to Bangkok wearing his first pair of shoes (his older brother's Bata sneakers) with fantasies of becoming a newsman. He lived in a *wat,* worked part time as a journalist, and attended night classes at Chulalongkorn and Thammasat Universities, but in time his marginal economic situation lead to illness, and the necessity for him to leave Bangkok. He then lived for five years as an isolated government forest ranger in Lamphun Province in the North where he thrived—psychologically, physically, and as a reader and writer.

Returning to Central Thailand, he worked on an anthropological research project with me and other American scholars, using his spare time to launch his career as a serious writer. When he needed money, he would take on odd jobs such as working as a traveling sewing machine salesman. With a colleague, he later bought a farm in Khorat Province which he turned into a successful modern operation producing corn, cotton, and, later, milk while his creative writing and increasing celebrity led to invitations to visit the United States, Europe, and Africa where he lectured at several universities on his own work and contemporary Thai literature. On two occasions in the early 1970s, he sold some of his cows to finance his unsuccessful efforts to be elected to the Thai parliament. But these failures did not prevent him from being hounded out of Thailand after the horrific 1976 murder of students at Thammasat University when an extreme right-wing government took over power in Thailand. He and his family spent the next two years as political refugees in Sweden which was perhaps the most depressing period of his life—not only because he was cut off from all that was culturally familiar, but because his language limitations and age inhibited him from seriously exploring Swedish culture. However, he did manage to work on a draft of a novel entitled *Cat,* the work being meant as a metaphor for Thailand. After a major change of government in Bangkok, Khamsing returned home to resume his old life as a modern farmer and writer.

In the intervening years Khamsing's literary stature has grown considerably, and in 1992 the National Culture Commission of Thailand officially selected him as a "National Artist of Thailand in Literature" which, among other things, is accompanied by a small annual stipend for the rest of his life. During the past decade, his early writings have been rediscovered by the young and are avidly read in both Thailand and Laos as a record of Thai rural life during the second half of the twentieth century.

Herbert P. Phillips

PRONUNCIATION GUIDE

The Thai words in this volume are romanized according to the Royal Institute system. A few of the Thai Buddhist terms are romanized using the generally accepted spellings, as are some names of historical people and places.

Below is an approximate pronunciation guide. In several cases, a single English spelling is used to represent more than one Thai sound.

CONSONANTS

Initial position:

K	S**K**IN
KH	**K**IN
P	S**P**IN
PH	**P**IN
T	S**T**ILL
TH	**T**ILL
CH	**J**AR; or **CH**IN
NG	SI**NG**
R	trilled 'r' sound

All other consonants are pronounced as in English.

VOWELS

A	ACROSS, FATHER
E	HEN, DAY
I	BIT, BEE
O	HOPE, SNOW; or SAUCE, SONG
U	BOOK, SHOE; or this 'u' sound said with a wide smile

AE	HAT
OE	FUR (without 'r' sound)
IA	INDIA
UA	JOSHUA; or wide 'u' + A
AI	ICE
AO	OUT
UI	COOING
OI	COIN
IU	FEW
EO	LAY OVER
OEI	OE + I (as in FUR and BEE)
UAI	UA + I (as in JOSHUA and BEE); or wide 'u' + A + I
AEO	AE + O (as in HAT and HOPE)
IEO	IA + O (as in INDIA and HOPE, similar to CLEOPATRA)

THE POLITICIAN

นักกานเมือง

THE shadows of the soaring pines falling across the rough road had shrunk in size to a couple of yards. The marketplace was quiet as usual at this time of the day. Once in a while a bicycle passed. Under the overhanging roofs thickly coated with dust a few country folk were walking. Now and again shouts emerged from the cafe on the corner but the passers-by paid no attention. Everyone knew that if there were anyone who might be tipsy any time any season, it could only be Khoen or, as he was known around town, Professor Khoen, and his three or four hangers-on.

To tell the truth, they weren't a bad bunch. If rowdy, it was usually when each had drunk enough to be stewed, and Khoen, their leader, wasn't a debauched outsider. On the contrary, he had risen to be abbot of the local temple. He had reached the second of the three levels of dharma studies, his religious duties were well performed, and he was respected by the faithful. Had he remained in orders, it is not impossible he would have risen to be chief monk of the district. But alas, nothing is permanent. The belief of the devout, especially devout women, in the Sacred Teaching often becomes in time belief in a particular monk. When that happens, if the religiously inclined woman doesn't become a nun, the monk finds some reason to put aside the yellow robe.

Abbot Khoen was no exception. Among the devout women who enjoyed going to the temple, but not to listen to preaching,

1

was a widow named Wan Im. Before long, as everyone expected, the abbot left monastery and robe and moved into Wan Im's house where it was understood that they lived together as husband and wife. They lived quietly for some years but then, though her heart was unwilling, sickness took Wan Im away. Grief converted the former prelate. The sorrow, instead of dissipating in heavy drink as he had hoped, swelled. Several times people saw him weep aloud in the middle of the marketplace.

His wife's financial status having been assured from lending out money since she was young, Khoen had enough for food and liquor for a long time to come. Later, when Khwan and Koi, disciples from the days when he was a monk, joined him, the ex-abbot became the chief of the band the townsfolk characterized as "long-time monks, big-time louts."

The three had been drinking clear raw whiskey since morning. Gentle conversation grew bolder with the heat of the sun and intensified when Koet, janitor of the provincial administration building, drifted into the circle. "Professor, you've no idea just what a mess the country is in. Phibun and Phao[1] have flown off to goodness knows where," he said as he pulled a stool up to the table. The three turned to him attentively.

"It's a big mess all right," Koi mumbled drunkenly. "Maybe this is what the bigmouths were blowing about at election time. What did they say, Professor?" he said, poking his face at Khoen. "Cracy, cracy something."

"Democracy, you nut! Not 'cracy,'" Khoen said severely, "They call it a 'democratic coup d'etat' see. You have to have a lot of coups d'état. Otherwise it isn't democracy." He continued showing off his knowledge. "You're stupid. If you don't know, keep quiet. I know because at the last election the district officer

1. Field Marshal Phibunsongkhram and Police Gen. Phao Siyanon, fled the country after a public uprising set off by a rigged election.

2

and provincial governor came to me on bended knees begging me to be a chief canvasser for their boss."

"Eh, that's true!" Khwan put in. "The professor and I really gave it to them, No one had the nerve to speak. Now there's going to be another election of people's representatives, isn't there?" he added gleefully.

Koet put the glass down, brought his stool closer to the table, and nodded two or three times in assent. "Election for sure. I heard the bunch up at the provincial office spreading it around that it was time to get some service points again by going out and having the people knuckle to."

The wind puffed a cloud of red dust from the road into the shophouse. Falling pine needles pattered onto the tin roof.

"I have an idea," Koi spoke up again. "Since they need representatives, why don't you run, Professor?"

"Ha! You've got something there," Koet backed him up.

Koi, gathering enthusiasm, half stood up from his stool and continued in a loud voice, "Because . . . um . . . because the professor is a great man. He has money and no children to worry him. Wealth is corrupting, so why hang on to it? That's dead right, isn't it Khwan?"

The person questioned agreed with a slow nod of his head.

"Easy, dammit. You're looking for trouble," Khoen turned to him annoyed.

"They say these representatives are really big. Bigger than village heads; bigger than county chiefs, bigger than district officers, bigger than provincial governors, and what really matters, bigger than the police. Now that's it. You can do anything. Booze, beat up anyone, kick the Chinese in the pants. Who could stop you? You could get even with that bloody police sergeant Huat. Just yesterday we laced into each other at the poker game at the chief's house behind the police station."

Khoen listened intently to Khwan's gabble. He chuckled,

wagging his head like a tall bell scaffold swaying in the first storms of the rainy season. He muttered, "This here Khwan doesn't know what he's talking about. I used to be a vote-getter for the provincial governor.[2] I know that anyone who gets to be a representative has to be an important person, really knowledgeable about money matters." He paused for a second to reach for his glass of whisky, then took a gulp. "Even as we are, people say we're bad. You know, if it wasn't because I have some money and did some bullying to help the big guys at the last election, by now the police would have done me in." He fixed his eyes on Khwan. "I can't even be a decent person myself, how could I represent anybody else?"

"That's not right, Professor. I think to be a representative nowadays you've got to be a hooligan, shout a lot, and put people off by cursing their families right back to their great grandfathers. You saw the bunch running for office last time: no better than us ruffians, shouting around, swearing in the middle of the street. Even if we are a little wild, there are only a few of us. That last crowd of representatives brought in a pack of thieves, hundreds of them. That's why I think the professor would be a great representative."

"It's not easy. I used to be a canvasser. I know."

"That's it. That's just it! You can be a vote-getter for others. What makes you think you can't be a vote-getter for yourself? Give it a try, Professor, give it a try." He patted Khoen on the back. "If anything goes very wrong, we'll punch them up. So what? Our fists are pretty well known around here."

"But . . ." The voice of the professor softened. "But what will I say to them? I hear those people hungry for office blabbering,

2. Provincial governors were not elected but it was common practice for the party in power to get governors to recruit canvassers to insure election of the government party candidates.

lying, and boasting of a million and one things. People like me, even if I am a drunk . . . I was a monk. I studied. If you want me to lie and crow, well, it sticks in my throat."

Khwan called for some more whisky. The whooshing of the wind across the tin roof blotted out the whistling of the pines. Whisky gurgled faintly into the glasses. At almost the same moment, each of the four reached for his and drank. Their expressions and eyes were thoughtful.

"Golly," Khwan groaned softly, "Professor, you're making too much of this. How hard can it be? I could be elected if I had the money. You lambaste them. You can point your finger in their faces and give them hell."

"If things go wrong, we'll smash them into the ground," Koi interjected. "We're local people. The folks around know what we can do. The odds are with us. Put up a fight. Look, Professor, the more they say these representatives are bigger than the police, the more it's worth a go. How many times has Sergeant Huat pushed us around? Maybe it's our turn now."

Outside the shop, the sun was dazzling. The gray gravel covering the road reflected the light like the scales of those plaster serpents decorating temple steps. Bicycles were passing by. Khoen stared down the road that thrust straight into the dense forest. The surrounding mountains were faintly visible in the flames of sunshine. His head nodded drunkenly again as a dark green bicycle steadily approached.

"Eh, if it isn't Sergeant Huat." Khoen popped to his feet. "Hey Sarg, I'm a representative. What do you think of that!"

Bicycle brakes screeched. "Drunk again. Go home. Making a commotion, disturbing the people. I'll haul you off to the police station in a minute."

Crestfallen, Khoen dropped back on to his bench staring after the gray shirt until it disappeared around a corner at the end of the marketplace.

"That's the ticket, Professor," a voice piped up. "This isn't the first time Sergeant Huat's bit the dust."

"In fact we take turns. Sometimes him, sometimes me," Khoen mused faintly.

The news that Mr. Khoen Khianrak, more commonly known as Professor Khoen, would run for election as a people's representative spread quickly from the market at the beginning of the road right up to the provincial administration building. Government officials split their sides with laughter but the common folk knew only that a candidate had to be obliging and generous and good at passing out whisky, cigarettes, and even money, and had to like talking loud about things no one knew anything about, and well . . . Professor Khoen seemed fully qualified.

On the day fixed for the registration of candidates, accompanied by Khwan, Koi, and Koet, Khoen filed his papers. No difficulties were encountered. Khoen paid the deposit of three thousand baht and handed in a number of photographs taken when he had just left the monastery. From that day on, the little marketplace of this frontier province perked up. Cars of various shapes and sizes managed to make their way to the province and helter-skeltered from one corner of the town to the other. For this election, there were almost ten candidates including former government officials, lawyers, titled bigwigs, and grand city folks, most of them from the capital and neighboring provinces. Only Khoen was a native of the province.

The expectation of handouts of money, whisky, tobacco, and food established by the last crop of candidates and the lack of farming to be done because it was the dry season brought a heavy stream of people down from the distant hills. The numbers grew with the approach of election day. Night after night the candidates showed their movies, some nights only one show taking place, but on others as many as three stands would compete with one another. Candidates proclaimed their virtues as though they were supermen. The crowds milled around noisily from group to group watching to see if anything was being given away and if disappointed would move on to another circle. It seemed even more festive than the annual fair.

Khoen and his cronies floated drunkenly with the rest of the crowd. He didn't have a chance to make speeches and if he did, wouldn't have known what to say. The most he could manage was to make disturbances as things went along. But that didn't go over so well because the people, still hoping the candidates would hand out money and fearing Khoen would jeopardize the opportunity, became menacing. One night, two groups of candidates set up their platforms, projectors, and screens in different corners of the field. Each of the office-seekers boasted of his boldness, ability, honors, infinite qualifications. Some boasted of having built roads, wells, monasteries, and even lavatories. One volunteered to construct houses, plant gardens, build schools and hospitals. The people looked on with interest. Khoen invited four or five buddies to start shouting from nearby.

"NO GOOD! SHUT UP! NONSENSE! NO . . ." Before he finished, Khoen realized he was flat on his back from the force of somebody's fist to which was added a growl, "We're all waiting for money so what the hell are you shouting for?"

Khoen, dejected, his mouth and ears swollen, an eye closed, staggered towards home with his friends. "It looks bad," he muttered to his cronies while swaying down the road. That night all except Khoen slept in a stupor. The force of the blow earlier that evening forced his mind to search for a way to get the better of them. He rubbed his mouth and groaned softly, but before dropping off to sleep, smiled.

At dawn, Khoen, still groggy, got up and staggering a few steps forward stumbled over Khwan, kicking him lightly in the middle of the back.

"Khwan, get up, get up Khwan."

Khwan turned over and bracing himself with both hands against the floor reached a sitting position but then fell over again. On the third try he stayed up and squinted about. "You sure are skinny, Professor," he mumbled while fishing about for a water bowl. "Must be from too much drink and not enough sleep."

"None of your flattery. Nothing physical is permanent."

Khwan pulled Koi up from his sleep. The cloudless morning was chilly, the mist tumbling with the pale sunshine.

Khoen looked at his two followers, his eyes showing fatigue. "Koi, Khwan," he started slowly, "I have found the way to do the loud mouths in. I know that most of the crowd have come because they think money is going to be handed out." He stroked the still swollen parts of his face. "So you two go around the marketplace and tell everyone that if they want to get money, come to my house. Tell them I'll take them to get the money myself."

As soon as his henchmen were out of the house, Khoen went back to sleep. Later in the day he awoke, delighted to find the house was filled with noise and people. He tiptoed over to a crack in the wall to peep out at them: a real crowd, even more than he expected. His face dirty, his clothes wrinkled from sleeping, he stepped outside. Khwan and Koi led the people with two loud hurrahs. The people echoed them with a roar. Khoen shouted at the top of his voice, "All right, all right, my brethren." Interest focused. "Now, there are a number of good people out there with money. They come here wanting to be our representatives." A brief pause to gather breath. "They all say they can do everything, build everything. Some of them say they're going to build roads, dig canals, or build us schools. Things like that they can do." Brief pause. "But compare those things to money, which do we want?" For an instant the question hung in the air.

"We want money, we want the money, money, money moneeee," the cry resounded through the crowd.

"Good, very good. But we've got to go and get the money from them. They can build streets and roads. They need money to do it. They must have money. Where are they, where are they?" he asked provocatively.

"At the hotel, they're at the hotel, the lot of them," returned the shouts from the crowd.

"All right, let's go!" Khoen jumped from the porch, but fell over on his face from the exhaustion of the previous night's adventures, arms and legs askew in a billow of dust and drawing a good laugh from the mob. He got up quickly, brushed the dust off, and strode resolutely in front. A thousand people stretched in a long turbulent procession behind him heading for the small hotel, the only one in town.

Seeing a herd of people approaching, the group at the hotel, with politicians' instinct, scurried to dress themselves as befits their dignity. Some, quickly pinning on their medals and decorations, in full dress, throats twitching, gave orders to their people to connect the loudspeakers. "Hey, hurry up, looks like they're really coming this way. See what I mean. The stupidity of the people really pays; it's like a pot of gold." Some jumped from their beds and began practicing gestures for their speeches.

Villagers, who had no idea of what was going on, carried and dragged their kids along into the crowd. The whole body of astonished government officials dropped their work to look on from the sides. The candidates formed a line in front of the hotel. Khoen walked straight to them.

"We want to come to an agreement with you honorable representatives," he began.

"With great pleasure," the oldest one replied, bowing until his body looked like an old shrimp at the end of the rainy season. "If there is anything at all we can do for you, we will, to the best of our ability, speak up for you." A broad smile pushed out his ruddy jowls as he led the whole group in a bow.

"What have you got to give us?"

"Whatever the people of our province desire, whatever will serve the welfare of the people of our province, that will I do for my fellows until my last breath," spoke up a young one at the end of the row winding up with a little bow which brought the others down in little bows.

Without hesitation, Khoen yelled at his loudest, "MONEEE, WE WANT MONEY!"

The crowd took up Khoen's cry. "Money, we've come for money!" The words reverberated over and over again. "Money, money!"

The candidates fidgeted. Some began to sweat. Some tried to state their policies and aims. Some began to tout their own past activities and offered plans for the future. But the increasing demand for money prevented them all from finishing. The old noble who had dragged his shriveled body up from the capital fainted to the delighted cheers of the crowd. Those who tried to speak crumpled their notes in frustration. The cries grew deafening as Khoen firmly made his way to the microphone and gestured to the mass. "All you faithful, you've seen for yourselves that they're a lot of wind. They'll do everything for us, but how can they do anything when all we do is ask for money and they don't have any to give us? When that's the way it is, how can we believe them? How can we elect them?" His voice was emphatic. "These fellows who are running for office come from different ranks and classes. That one over there is a knight." He pointed his finger. "The next one over there is a sir. And the one next to him is a lawyer. The old one there who almost died a minute ago is a noble. That one there who's hung a lot of magic charms on his chest is a general. All you faithful, decide for yourselves who you are going to elect. Now I used to be a canva . . . er, that is,

I used to go to Bangkok. Now I'll tell you something. A lot of you probably don't know what a knight, a sir, and so forth, are. Well, I'll tell you. A knight looks after horses and also sometimes feeds and waters chickens, ducks, and elephants. They do it at night. I know because I've been to Bangkok. A sir we ought to speak to as "Sire," and we know that sires are kept for our mares that don't have any foals yet. As for this noble, I have my doubts about him. What kind of noble doesn't wear his proper robes? Maybe he's an ignoble noble." He paused to swallow.

"That one over there who loves those toys is a general. Take a look. Pinning a row of seashells on his chest! Those people are childish. They like toys just like our children. The one who's sneaking away, he's a lawyer, someone who likes trouble where he finds it. No money to give him and you land in jail."

The crowd listened in astonished silence. Khoen was still for an instant and then continued.

"Dear friends, the others have done a lot of talking. Today, listen to me. I'm a candidate too. Who was it a little while ago who said he really knows us, really knows our poverty and troubles? Ask him, brethren, ask him. Does he know how many acres we have? Does he know what we eat with our rice in the morning? Believe me, he doesn't know. Empty talk. Now take me. I'll do anything you want. Kick a dog, bash somebody's head in. Anyone you don't like, you tell me. Er . . . uh." As his eyes lit on Sergeant Huat standing at the side, his voice tempered. "What I just said . . . in fact I never did anything like that. I'll end here. Amen. May you have long life, good looks and health, and may the Triple Gem help me become a people's representative."

From that day, Khoen's reputation flourished among the people while the other candidates dodged public meetings to avoid the taunts. Some, losing their nerve, fled back to Bangkok.

Election day came and passed without incident. The official

results were announced a little past eight in the evening. Soon after, Sergeant Huat rushed breathlessly up to the duty officer at the police station.

"Now I'm in for it, sir," the poor policeman gasped. "Mr. Khoen, he was drunk and raising a row in the market. I locked him up here since morning and now he's the people's representative. I'm not going to be in this district for long, that's for sure." His voice was tinged with alarm.

"That's bad. That's really bad. Have you released him yet?" the duty officer asked, lifting his eyes from the daily reports. But Sergeant Huat had already vanished.

The duty officer then walked over and opened the cell door. The three of them were sprawled on the floor sleeping. The stench of vomit mixed with other filth wafted out. Locating Khoen, the officer reached out to shake him gently but swiftly withdrew his hand when he found his target covered with vomit. He grumbled to himself and used his foot instead, nudging Khoen lightly.

"Sir, sir, mister, hey Khoen, Khoen."

"Huh," Khoen drawled. "Where am I? Give me some water." He screwed up his eyes. "Black as pitch."

"It's night already. You can leave, sir. Please wake up those two gentlemen."

"Eh, who are you talking to, Lieutenant?" Khoen asked bewildered.

"I'm talking to the honorable representative, sir. Please leave. The election is over now."

Khoen took some time to wake up the other two, and then all three crawled outside. Each drank a bowl of water offered by the police, walked unsteadily out of the police station, and disappeared in the darkness. Khoen still kept to himself the news heard a moment before from the police. His ears were ringing with the words "honorable representative" spoken with humility by the authorities who had for so long bullied him. The three bumbled through the blackness in silence and crawled up the stairs to the house. Khwan and Koi flopped down at once and went back to sleep by the stairs. Khoen rested, his brain agitated but confused. The drunkenness had vanished. He felt airy, as if disembodied. He began to think of things he had never thought of before, of the words "people's representative." He thought of what Koet said in the cafe. "A representative is bigger than the district officer, bigger than the provincial governor." Apart from that he knew nothing. Was that all? Doubt welled. Surely there was something more because he knew that every people's representative had to go to Bangkok. But they must have more to do than just go to the capital. Khoen began to reflect on Bangkok and its crazy bigness. Didn't this mean he had to go there to live, separated from his own people in a different kind of life? Now what would that be like? The outlook wasn't bright any more. Khoen had been to Bangkok once when still a monk. He tried to recall the name of the temple where he had stayed but couldn't. The failure preyed on his mind. Anxiety increased as he recollected a picture of a previous representative cloaked outlandishly in a jacket that looked like a whole blanket, with a silly rag dangling from his neck. He mumbled to himself, "What a fool. You don't know when you're well off."

The moon and constellations sank in the sky. "Whew, this world is sure getting hot for me," he exclaimed to himself. As he went to get a drink of water, the neighbor's roosters crowed their announcement of dawn. Khoen was afraid of the daybreak. Bleakness was creeping in with it. The bushes and trees were beginning to have an outline. In that instant he made up his mind. Khwan and Koi were dead asleep. He disappeared into the house for a second and returned, casting a glance and a sigh at his two disciples. Finally, he tiptoed past them, went out of the house, and headed straight for the marketplace, like a mechanical doll, with but one thought in mind: to go. At the head of the road at the end of the market area he saw a standing truck and heard three people making a noise, so he drifted over. Two young fellows faced him as if he were some night pilferer but beckoning asked for a hand to push the stalled vehicle. In a few words Khoen learned that the truck was carrying rice and other goods across the border. He helped at once and in a second the engine fired and the truck disappeared in the direction of the glow on the horizon.

No one saw Mr. Khoen again. No one in the province knew where he had gone. Those who knew turned out to be the reporters from the Bangkok newspapers. Several of the papers ran the story that a fearless representative of the people had his mouth closed by a dark power and that his body was thrown over a cliff for the vultures to pick at. A photo of vultures circling under white clouds accompanied the news item.

Now the little province is busy again. Every day fancy cars of the big boys from Bangkok investigating this mysterious case arrive and take back to the city a policeman or two. One car just went off this morning carrying away Sergeant Huat muttering, "Damn, now I've had it."

1958

BREEDING STOCK

คนพันธุ์

THE hand of the old woman shook a bit as she stretched up to pick a ripening gourd from the top of the fence. Just one more, she thought, would be enough for supper. On the second try she caught it, the plump one she wanted. A smile like the fresh breeze of the cool season lit her face as she muttered to herself how fast they grew. Only three months before, her husband had thrust a few brown seeds into her hand with instructions to plant them at the base of the bamboo fence and now, barely the end of the rainy season, the picket surrounding the house had become an arbor trellised with gourd vines, their yellow flowers interspersing the young light green vegetables, like pieces of gold leaf, with the carpenter bees and the honey bees that she liked to watch journeying from one flower to another. Day by day she saw with happy pride how her vines grew until now they concealed every trace of the bamboo stakes. She could not help but cast her eyes around the compound from the vines to the sesbans and the mango trees. All were the fruit of her own hand. Those sesban plants with their delicious flowers which only the year before carried reddish tops and sickly leaves, this year surpassed the roof of the house. She took comfort in them when she was alone.

She often thought of the changes around her: of her own children who, like birds whose wings had grown strong and legs firm, went their own way, some far, some near. Often when asked how many children she had, she would say five but

15

sometimes she said it with a little inward laugh when she recalled that in fact she had had seven altogether. The first child died when it was still in that limbo between the world of spirits and the world of man and she neither felt regret nor had the temerity to count it as one of her own. Although, then terribly weak from the difficult labor, she remembered well the tiny infant that was born of the spirits, her husband's exclamation, "Oh, a boy, we have a boy!" and the faint incanting of the middle-aged herbal doctor—"Spirits, if it's yours take it now; from tomorrow on it's mine"—finally obscured by the crying of the child. Halfway through the night when she had been bathed in warm water and comfortably put by the hot fire, her husband and friends came to tell her that the baby had already died. So much for the child. The woman, lacking the courage to look at it again, let them quietly dispose of the flesh of her flesh. The herbalist told her that they could not fight the previous mother who had caught up with the infant and taken him back. She knew that the mother they referred to was a spirit and felt fear rather than sadness, firmly believing that the child was the spirit's and not hers.

Many years later another died, such a lovable boy of six, but this time the woman grieved, the tears flowing until there were no more. Her friends and relatives consoled her by saying that it was the child's own fate, its karma, that determined the child was to live in the world with them only until that time, and that its accumulated merit was simply exhausted. The woman thought about it and half believed them but the tears continued to flow. "What kind of fate was it that singled out my child to die of chickenpox? Why didn't the children of other women suffer the same fate?" When they were taking away the body of the child, the woman impulsively snatched up her betel box and with the red lime in it made a mark on the lifeless breast, sobbing, "Be born of your mother again my baby, oh, my baby, your mother is making a mark here, here."

Then the body was wrapped in an old mat and carried from her. The woman had many other children, boys and girls, but as none showed a red birthmark on the breast, belief that the dead child's merit really did last only for as many years as he had lived gradually dissipated the sorrow. The remaining children were raised with great care and love and when they grew up they left her. The last one, a daughter, went off to live with her husband just at planting season that very year.

After giving some bran to the pigs and chickens, she went up into the house to boil the young gourds and make shrimp paste and chili sauce and fix two handfuls of beans, just enough for supper. Then she went out to the front landing of the house to wait for her husband. The sesban leaves had closed in the misty dusk and the woman reflected that while she had a mother, a father, sisters, brothers, and her very own children, all had gone their ways leaving her again alone with her husband who, after all, was not her kin, but still the only person who was really hers. She was proud of him, so good and industrious he was.

Others agreed. The previous year the authorities from the district office came to their house and praised her and her husband so much that while she forgot some of the things they said, she did remember they said her husband was one of the hardest workers of the district and that he should go to the district office to receive an award the government was going to give him. Early the following morning her husband left and returned just before dark carrying a little shiny cup and a young chicken. He boasted to his wife that it was a prize cup made of silver sent from Bangkok. Bewildered, she studied it for she could not understand how the little whitish thing could be a cup. She questioned her husband but he assured her it really was and even insisted she take good care of it because the district officer told him it was very valuable and he should keep it safely.

But still she didn't understand. Often wondering what it was

17

for, she speculated that maybe the people of Bangkok had a different kind of shrimp paste and chili sauce that needed this funny kind of cup, but even so why didn't the district officer give her husband a real cup she could use for the sauce? She would secretly show it to the neighbors but none of them could tell her what it was really for. Some of them thought that from the shape of it, it was probably meant to be used for water for the chickens and she tended to agree, because on the day her husband brought it, he also brought a young chicken telling her it was a breeding chicken given by America. He went on to say that they would have to become up to date because the country was advancing, for proof of which he pointed to the chicken that he said had to be ordered from America.

He exaggerated a bit. "When this chicken is full grown it will be only a little smaller than a vulture. What do you think of that! The authorities said our Thai chickens are out of date, too small and the price is no good, so we have to get roosters from America."

She listened with some anxiety thinking that her chickens were going to be the size of vultures. She closed her eyes trying unsuccessfully to imagine what her house on stilts would be like with a flock of enormous fowl running around underneath it. She would miss the pretty sight in the mornings and evenings of her nice mottled and multicolored chickens. Still, she didn't feel she should voice her misgivings and marveled to herself at the progress and changes going on. As time passed, her husband's frequent accounts of the oddities of progress finally brought her around to enjoying tales of what she never thought could be in this world.

When many days later the officials from the district came again to hold a meeting at the local temple, she waited for a long time, hoping her husband would come back with new stories to tell. And so he did. With a look of amusement, he told his wife that the agriculture officer called the meeting to announce that America had sent some breeding pigs and that they were to send their sows to the district center to be serviced. So the following dawn he went off taking their sow, leaving his wife to her thoughts the whole day, but for the life of her she couldn't imagine who America was. When her husband returned, his description was extravagant as usual.

"It's really only a little smaller than our own water buffalo," he related with pride.

The poor woman's trepidation grew because if the pigs really became buffaloes then what would she do? Not sure whether he was talking about buffaloes or pigs, she asked him which he meant.

"Pigs, of course," he affirmed.

"All right, but what do they eat, grass or bran?" she asked, still doubting.

Her husband, a little perplexed, replied with a chuckle, "Well, I suppose they eat bran."

Another day it happened again. Her husband left the house early together with their cow. The evening before, the county chief sent a man over to tell them that America had sent breeding cattle but it was a long time before she realized he meant a bull and wondered just how big it would be. She waited the whole day for her husband, anxious to hear what he would have to say. Just before dark, she knew from the sound of the wedge being driven in to hold the fence gate shut that her husband had returned. It was the same sound she had heard from the time they were both young, a firm vigorous sound then but now the pounding of the mallet on the wedge told her that her husband was becoming an old man.

"Giants they were, both the bull and the man," he said excitedly. "Enormous!"

While setting out the food, the woman listened to the story.

"As big as I don't know what. At first I thought it was a buffalo but then I looked at it and looked at it and there it was, a bull. Its hooves, its legs, horns, ears, all like a bull but what a size!" he said between mouthfuls.

"The agriculture officer said that the government ordered these bulls from America because our own cows are good for nothing. They are old-fashioned, grow slowly, no good for food or work. And I suppose he's right." The last sentence was offered as his own opinion and he didn't stop talking throughout supper.

"I've lived to see the day! I have seen an American. With my own eyes I saw him. The size of him! Like this."

He turned to where his wife was sitting.

"Eh, what can I compare him with so that you can get an idea? I know. You've seen a scarecrow, haven't you?"

"I have," she agreed.

"Well, he was like that: all arms and legs with hazel eyes just like our own dog's eyes, and hair yellow-brown like dried grass. I was standing close to him and he was saying some gibberish full of words like "kay kay" and I don't know what. With him was a Thai, a very crude man. I don't know what they were saying except for that word *'yet'*[1] that no decent person would use, but he kept repeating it."

She went to bed early but couldn't fall asleep for thinking about the story she had heard that evening. She closed her eyes and saw the scarecrow in the corner of the paddy field with its long arms, long legs, big head, cloaked in a tattered old monk's robe, hung so that the wind would blow it back and forth to chase the sparrows, but she couldn't see how it could be like this American. Was it true? But she knew her husband hadn't lied to her before. Still, it was terribly hard to believe him. Then there was something more she wanted to ask her husband. She started

1. A pun: Thais have difficulty in pronouncing the final "s" so that the word "yes" sounds like *"yet,"* which is a crude Thai equivalent to "fuck."

20

out past the door where he was sitting, the red glow from his hand-rolled banana leaf cheroot illuminating the darkness. Suddenly feeling ashamed of the thought in her head, she went back inside. A little later her husband came inside, brushed the sleeping mat with a few flicks of a cloth, and lay down beside her. The cheroot still glowed periodically. She thought for a long time and finally couldn't resist putting the question.

"Grandpa," she addressed her husband as did her grand-children.

"What is it?" her husband answered quietly while crushing out the cheroot against the wall.

"Why did they send the scarecrow over?"

"Uh," her husband sighed deeply.

"They sent him for breeding just like the bull, didn't they?" she asked further.

There was silence for a moment. "I guess so. That must be it. That must be why the Thai man was using that smutty word all day long."

"And are they sending him to our district?"

"Not yet I think. Now they're just using him in Bangkok for the women there," he replied, tickled by the idea.

"Oh!"

"What do you mean by 'Oh'?" her husband queried.

"Oh, erh, that is, I feel sorry for, well, I feel sorry for those Thai cows, that's all Grandpa," she faltered.

"Well, for the Thai people, too."

The last sentence hardly disturbed the stillness of the dark night.

1958

QUACK DOCTOR
หมอเถื่อน

HE recalled having seen the young man from a distance four or five months before. The outfit was the same, olive-green trousers, a pale blue-red shirt like the sky at dusk, dark glasses and a small black leather case. The kids around identified him as a quack doctor but what with the world filled with so many strange new things he couldn't guess what kind of a doctor was a "quack." The month before, the village headman actually brought two doctors from the town to take care of some water buffaloes, of all things, dying of the plague. From that event he added to his stock of general knowledge that there were now even buffalo doctors, cow doctors, pig doctors, and dog doctors. As he thought maybe those two water buffalo doctors were, as people said, quack doctors, the next time he saw them in the middle of a field he asked them unabashed: "Boys, the two of you there are quack doctors, aren't you?"

Instead of replying, they upbraided him for lacking respect and a lot of other things, which left him no wiser as to what a quack doctor might be. He watched the two disappear huffily, and when his son-in-law passed by on his way to his paddy field, asked him hesitantly, "What does a quack doctor actually do?"

"They treat people like us, what did you think?" the son-in-law replied impatiently. But when his father-in-law remained incredulously silent, he added, "Their medicine is pretty damn good. You can be shivering out your teeth with malaria and with one shot, you're sitting up. Look at Old Man Si, he'd already told his children and grandchildren to start sawing planks for his coffin when they gave him one injection and now he's eating like a horse."

"They give injections, do they?" the old man mused. "Then they're the same as the water buffalo doctors, ain't they?"

The son-in-law, not being sure himself, neither agreed nor disagreed, only smiled.

His father-in-law, Grandpa Sa, son of the soil, always having to do with buffaloes and cattle, marveled at the fantastic abilities of these doctors and couldn't help thinking of Grandma Ma, his helpmate through thick and thin. "She must have been short on merit not to have lived to see the coming of the quack doctors," he lamented. "A little fever did her in while Old Man Si has recovered after nearly dying goodness knows how many times."

This year Sa was seventy. His skin sagged on his frame but he was still strong enough to get around a little in the neighborhood. He had many children and grandchildren, all but two of whom had moved away. His youngest son and daughter, both of them married and living in houses built close together, remained. Not being rich, both children still worked the small rice field, sharing whatever could be harvested. The old man lived in one house for a time, and then shifted to the other, helping out by doing whatever odd jobs he could manage. Apart from looking after the children, he watched over the houses when no one else was there. This gave him a little self-esteem sometimes amounting to happiness. At first, when Smokey, their only dog, disappeared and was found dead at the edge of the field (the children said poisoned by the thieves), he was dismayed but soon got over it thinking it was just as well because it gave him the chance to be a real help to his family now that he alone had to watch the houses. On the day Smokey disappeared, thieves did take nearly all the chickens from his son's coop. "Never mind, son, if they're gone, they're gone. From now on, your father will do Smokey's job," he volunteered.

His son and son-in-law together built him a little shelter at the entrance to the water buffalo pen and from then on, practically the whole night through, the neighbors would hear the old man pounding his betel or coughing.

"If we're going to stand in for the dog, we'll have to do it at least as well," he thought. "Whenever a dog hears anything suspicious, he barks. Now we can't bark but a little throat clearing should do as well. Ahem, Ahem."

Although the old man's coughing got hoarser and fainter with the passage of time, he felt that through habit he was improving. Sometimes the simple turning over of a buffalo would set off his "Ahem, ahem," the quick reaction of his tongue and throat pleasing him greatly. But as time went on, Grandfather Sa felt weak on his legs and would doze frequently. Some nights he would start up when a quid of betel he was chewing would slide unexpectedly into his throat. Food, which once seemed so tasty, wouldn't go down.

The young man approached the porch of the house slowly and smiled. The old man hesitated for a minute wondering what to say.

"What brings you here, young fellow?" he greeted him.

"I was just looking at my patients in that house over there." He pointed to the house, his answer letting the old man know he was a doctor. "Wouldn't you like to have some medicine handy, Uncle?" Without waiting for a reply, he climbed the steps up to the house, put his square case next to him, removed his sun-glasses, folded them, and put them into his shirt pocket.

"Well, doctor, what kind of medicine do you have? Do you have something to give me an appetite?"

"Yes, I've got everything you want, Uncle, just tell me what the trouble is and I can give you the right kind of medicine."

"Well, now, it's like this," he began. "Three nights ago I was having pains in my throat, lost my voice, and halfway through the night my heart felt fluttery. Sometimes I drop off to sleep and I can't eat or drink anything."

"Umm," the young man murmured. "That means you haven't been getting very much sleep."

"Well, I did doze off a few times."

"Turn around, Uncle," he instructed.

As the old man turned his back, he fumbled around in his bag. "Where have I left my instruments? Come a little closer." He thumped the old man's spine, then moved over to the ribs, as though he were tapping a hollow log. He knocked and listened over the whole back.

"Now, then, Uncle, turn around again." The old man complied obediently. "Open your mouth."

"Ahhhh," the old man sounded softly.

"Stick out your tongue. Now pull your lower eyelids down." Then he used the edge of his hand to tap on the old man's chest.

"My head doesn't feel right," the old man said, "you'd better tap that too. Maybe you'll find what's wrong there."

The doctor, smiling a little, knocked four or five times in the middle of his forehead.

"You're doing just like a farmer," the old man chuckled exposing his gums. "We tap just like that to tell whether a watermelon is ripe. If it's ripe it goes 'uk, uk,' or when we're looking for turnips to dig up, we pound the ground, and if it goes 'chu, chu,' you dig there and find one. What have you found wrong, doctor?"

"More than one thing," he replied seriously.

"Of course you did. It went 'pung, pung.'" He paused for a moment. "I don't have enough money, not if I've got a lot of things wrong. What there is belongs to the children. But they're all out in the paddy field."

25

"That's all right, Uncle, I'll give you three pills. Take one a day before going to bed. And tell your children I'll be back tomorrow."

The afternoon cloudiness later turned into a drizzle. The smoky fire, kindled to drive the mosquitoes from the buffalo pen, threw a reddish light. The sight of the albino buffalo stretching his head up while chewing its cud deliciously made the old man suddenly hungry for some betel. The rain drummed harder on the grass roof. The cooking fires in the houses of his daughter and son were extinguished. He was enveloped in darkness. While groping for the betel nut and clove leaves he'd already prepared, he remembered the medicine that had been given to him. "Almost forgot," he reproached himself while putting a tablet in his mouth. The slightly sweet taste excited him. Since his youth he'd heard it said that if a sick person finds medicine to his taste, then the medicine is right for the ailment and the sickness will soon be over. When he recalled his son-in-law saying that the medicine was damn good, he became even happier and completely forgot the instructions. He took another tablet, and it seemed the tiny pill was even sweeter. "There, it must be just right for what's wrong with me. It's nice and sweet." He put the third into his mouth. "Go away now, trouble. Just let me get my appetite back."

"Ahem, ahem," the old man's voice sounded sleepy in the chill night air.

Late the next morning, his son, daughter, son-in-law, daughter-in-law all called out, tearfully, "Pa, the buffalo is gone, Pa!"

The daughter was the first to make a commotion when, glancing over to the pen, she saw it was empty. "The whole fence on the east side is down. Thieves have got the buffalo," she called out. They all rushed to the enclosure. "With the buffalo gone, where are we going to get any rice to eat?" his son raged. "The

26

paddy field is filled with water, we've already pulled up the seedlings for transplanting; what are we going to plough with?" But when they looked over at the open shelter at the entrance to the pen they were flabbergasted. The soft sunlight illuminated the old man's face, his deep sunken eyes fast asleep. They all went over to him and found him snoring pleasantly. "Father, Father," the daughter shook him. "Pa, Father," they all cried at him furiously.

"Uh." He turned over sleepily.

"Pa, thieves have taken our buffalo," the daughter said, choked with tears.

"Uh," the old man managed drowsily.

The square leather bag swinging in time to his steps, he ambled over, his bright shirt blowing in the rainy mist still lingering in the soft sunlight. "How're things?" he called out smiling broadly. "Did Uncle get some sleep?" Everyone turned to look at him dumbly. "Did you get some sleep, Uncle?" He asked again as he approached. "Yesterday I gave you three sleeping pills." He grinned and looked straight at everyone.

"What!" the son exclaimed. "So it was sleeping pills! He gave something to Pa to put him to sleep. He's one of the thieves!" A thick stick of hard firewood crashed down on the back of the young man's neck. He spun and fell on his face, the small bag flying off in a different direction.

1958

THE GOLD-LEGGED FROG

เขียดขาคำ

THE sun blazed as if determined to burn every living thing in the broad fields to a crisp. Now and again the tall, straight, isolated *sabang* and shorea trees let go of some of their dirty yellow leaves. He sat exhausted against a tree trunk, his dark blue shirt wet with sweat. The expanse round him expressed total dryness. He stared at the tufts of dull grass and bits of straw spinning in a column to the sky. The whirlwind sucked brown earth up into the air casting a dark pall over everything. He recalled the old people had told him this was the portent of drought, want, disaster, and death, and he was afraid. He was now anxious to get home; he could already see the tips of the bamboo thickets surrounding the house far ahead like blades of grass. But he hesitated. A moment before reaching the shade of the tree he felt his ears buzz and his eyes blur and knew it meant giddiness and sunstroke. He looked at the soles of his feet blistered from the burning sandy ground and became indescribably angry—angry at the weather capable of such endless torture. In the morning the cold had pierced his bones, but now it was so hot he felt his head would break into pieces. As he recalled the biting cold of the morning, he thought again of his little son.

That very morning he and two of his small children went out into the dry paddy fields near the house to look for frogs for the morning meal. The air was chilly. The two children on either side of him shivered as they stopped to look for frogs hiding in the cracks

28

of the parched earth. Each time they saw two bright eyes in a deep crack, they would shout, "Pa, here's another one. Pa, this crack has two. Gold-legged ones! Hurry, Pa."

He had hopped from place to place as the voices called him, prying up the dry clods with his hoe. He caught some of the frogs immediately, but a few jumped away as soon as he began digging. It was the children's job to give chase and pounce on them. Some they got. Some jumped into other fissures, obliging him to pry up a new cake of earth. Besides the frog, if his luck were good, he would unearth a land snail or razor clam waiting for the rains. He would take these as well.

The air had started to warm and already he had had enough frogs to eat with the morning rice. The sound of drumming, the village chief's call for a meeting, had sounded faintly from the village. Vague anger again spilled over as his thoughts returned to that moment. If only he had gone home then, the poor child would be all right now. It was really the last crack. As soon as he had poked it, the ground broke apart. A fully-grown gold-legged frog as big as a thumb leaped past the older child. The younger raced after it for about twelve yards when it dodged into a deep hoofprint of a water buffalo. The child groped for it. And then he was shocked almost senseless by the trembling cry of his boy, "Pa, a snake, a snake bit my hand."

A cobra spread its hood, hissing. When finally able to act, the father with all his strength had slammed the handle of his hoe three times down onto the back of the serpent, leaving its tail twitching. He carried his child and the basket of frogs home without forgetting to tell the other to drag the snake along as well.

On the way back his son had cried softly and moaned, beating his chest with his fists and complaining he could not breathe. At home, the father summoned all the faith healers and herbalists whose names he could think of and the turmoil began.

"Chop up a frog and put it on the wound," a neighbor called out.

When another shouted, "Give him the toasted liver of the snake to eat," he hurriedly slit open the snake to look for the liver while his wife sat by crying. The later it got, the bigger the crowd grew. On hearing the news, all the neighbors attending the village chief's meeting joined the others. One of them told him he had to go to the district office in town that very day because the village chief told them the government was going to hand out money to those with five or more children, and he was one who had just five. It was a new shock.

"Can't you see my boy's gasping out his life? How can I *go?*" he cried resentfully.

"What difference will it make? You've called in a lot of doctors, all of them expert."

"Go, you fool. It's two hundred baht they're giving. You've never had that much in your whole life. Two hundred!"

"Pardon my saying it," another added, "but if something should happen and the boy dies, you'd be out, that's all."

"I won't go," he yelled. "My kid can't breathe and you tell me to go. Why can't they hand it out some other day? It's true I've never had two hundred baht since I was born, but I'm not going. I am not going."

"Jail," another interjected. "If you don't go, you simply go to jail. Whoever disobeyed the authorities? If they decide to give, you have to take. If not, jail."

The word "jail" repeated like that unnerved him, but still he resisted.

"Whatever it is, I said I'm not going. I don't want it. How can I leave the kid when he's dying?" He raised his voice. "No, I won't go."

"You go. Don't go against the government. We're subjects." He turned to find the village chief standing grimly at his side.

"If I don't go, will it really be jail?" he asked in a voice suddenly become hoarse.

"For sure," the village chief replied sternly. "Maybe for life."

That did it. In a daze, he asked the faith healers and neighbors to take care of his son and left the house.

He reached the district office almost at eleven and found some of his neighbors who had also come for the money already sitting in a group. They told him to address the old deputy district officer which he did.

"I am Mr. Nak Na-ngam, sir. I have come for the money, the many-children money."

The deputy district officer raised his fat face to stare at him for a moment, then spoke heavily. "Idiot, don't you have eyes to see people are working. Get out! Get out and wait outside."

"But, sir, my boy is dying . . ." However he cut himself short when he thought perhaps if the official suspected that his child might be dead there would be trouble. The deputy officer looked down at his paper and went on scribbling. Nak dejectedly joined the group outside. "All you do is suffer if you're born a rice farmer and a subject," he thought. "You're poor and helpless, your mouth gets stained from eating roots when the rice has run out, you're at the end of your tether and you turn to the authorities only to be put down."

The official continued to write as if there were no peasants waiting anxiously. A few minutes after twelve, he strode from the office but had the kindness to say a few words. "It's noon already. Time for a break. Come back at one o'clock for it."

Nak and his neighbors sat there waiting until one o'clock. The taciturn deputy on returning called them all to sit on the floor near him. He began by asking each of them why they had so many children. The awkward replies of the peasants brought guffaws from the other officials who turned to listen to the embarrassed answers. At last his turn came.

"Who is Mr. Nak Na-ngam?"

"I am sir," he responded with humility.

"And now, why do we have such a lot of children?"

Several people tittered.

"Oh, when you're poor, sir " he burst out, his exasperation uncontrollable.

"What the hell's it got to do with being poor?" the deputy officer questioned in a voice that showed disappointment with the answer.

"We're awful poor and no money to buy a blanket. So no matter how bad the smell is always, I gotta use my wife for a blanket and the kids just keep comin'."

Instead of laughter, dead silence, finally broken by the dry voice of the blank-faced deputy, "Bah! This joker uses his wife for a blanket."

The wind gusted again. The *sabang* and shorea trees threw off another lot of leaves. The spears of sunlight still dazzled him. The whirlwind still hummed in the middle of the empty rice field ahead. Nak left the shade of the tall tree and headed through the flaming afternoon sunshine towards his village.

"Hey, Nak . . ." The voice came from a group of neighbors passing in the opposite direction. Another topped it.

"You sure are lucky." The words raised his spirits. He smiled a little before repeating expectantly, "How am I lucky—in what way?"

"The two hundred baht. You got it, didn't you?"

"I got it. It's right here." He patted his pocket.

"What luck! You sure have good luck, Nak. One more day and you'd have been out two hundred baht."

1958

DUST UNDERFOOT

ไพร่ฟ้า

—1—

"Do you like me, Bua Kham?"

Her flawless face, tilted slightly, was perfectly still as if carved of Burmese amber jade and impervious to human speech. Her yellow and red beaded eardrops glinted in the soft sunlight and a spray of tiny orchids lay still in her jet-black hair.

"Tell me, do you like me?" he persisted, his deep voice carefully articulating the words in not quite fluent Northern dialect.

The willowy figure remained immobile, gazing along the curve of the river edging the hills.

"Well, do you? I have money, you know."

Roused from her reverie, she cocked her pretty face to hear better and looked at him as if she saw him for the first time.

The young man smiled shyly, his hand trembling as he rubbed it against the red, yellow, and green Olympic ring design on the front of his T-shirt.

"I really do, I think." His voice was hesitant.

Her full red lips parted slightly. "You do? Do you have a lot?"

The unexpected question stunned him momentarily and then, elated, he turned to me to ask, "Boss, how much money have I got? Tell me. Come on, tell me," he prodded, when I took my time to think about it.

"It's a fairly large sum, Intha. It must come to about seven or eight hundred baht."

Although my uncertainty as to how much he had deposited with me must have been evident, Intha seemed satisfied. His clear laughter made me feel glad for him and I settled down again on the fine sand.

The Mae Ping River then was fairly low, leaving sandy beaches and dunes stretching along both banks. Every afternoon, when work was done, we would get together relaxing on the soft sand, catching fish. At dusk, back from the forest, the girls of the village would go in convoy down to bathe and do their laundry, their shrill banter rising over the stream. It seems each of us had a part, which will fix the Mae Ping River in our minds for a long time. As for me, for the rest of my life I will not forget this tortuous river, not because I was overwhelmed by the view of the majestic mountains and gorgeous range of teak trees along its bank or because of a memorable past full of meaning, but because it was here that I witnessed a tremendous love, contemptuous arrogance, and human vengeance that ended in tragedy.

Before going further, let me tell you a little about us.

As a result of the turmoil of World War II, I had become what you might call an adventurer, roaming over the northern provinces, working at anything that turned up. One day, as my friend and I were hitching a ride to Chiang Mai in an ancient truck belonging to a politician who had a lucrative salt monopoly in the North, we met the forest manager for the Phanarat Timber Company, one of the big operators in these parts. He took to us and eventually asked us both to work for him. We seized the chance. That year the company was working the forest at Phayao. From Phayao, we shifted to Fang where my friend met a girl with a beautiful pearly complexion and decided to end his nomadic existence. I continued working and liked it. We finished the Fang concession, then moved to Chiang Dao,

34

Phrao, Mae Taeng, Mae Rim, and right on down the Mae Ping River. By the time we got to the Mae Ko Forest, I had been promoted from checking clerk to labor foreman. It was then that I learned that the Phanarat Timber Company belonged to a princely family in Bangkok.

Intha appeared while we were still in Phayao. The company had bought a big bull elephant in Kengtung, in Burma, whose owner, on delivering him to us, declared he was a good strong worker but was inclined to be nasty and only responded to his mahout.

"That little fellow is the only one who can make him behave," the owner said, pointing to a small dark-skinned adolescent, hair unkempt, swinging his feet up on the neck of the elephant.

"He's a boy from the Kamu tribe. You'd better take him on. At fifty baht a month, he's cheap."

We took his advice. I guess Intha then was not more than sixteen years old. He was solid and tough, with a squarish face, and like all hill tribe boys had grown up naturally. Few diseases had passed him by, from malaria to the smallpox that pitted his face. Spending most of the day on the back of his elephant, he had little time to mix with people but all of us admired his directness and pluck. Perhaps Intha and I spent more time together than with the others because each of us felt a little lonely. He came from the deep forest along the Mae Kok River without friends from the same village, unlike the other employees, and I from the distant capital in the Chao Phraya River basin. Most of the others had hometown friends to go around with after hours. So both of us would usually be at the camp with more time to talk than the others. Intha took a liking to me because I had new things to show off to him and give him. I liked Intha because he often had exotic stories to tell. One evening, Intha told me about his association with Phlai Thong, the elephant.

35

"I've been with Phlai Thong since he was so high," he said pointing to a middling size anthill. "I was hired to feed and train him from the time he was captured in the jungle. He loves me and wouldn't ever do me any harm. The first man who bought him couldn't get him to do anything, so they had to take me on to manage him. I can't remember how many times he's been sold, but every time they have to sell me with him." Intha chuckled in good spirits. "We've never been apart. As long as Phlai Thong is alive, I won't go home."

Workers came and went but Intha and I continued on. I admired his tough spirit and he gave me complete respect and loyalty. When work was done, we would usually go around together. By now Intha had outgrown the boy who did not bother about girls, and liked to talk about them. Especially after we had come to Ko, it seemed as if he'd set his heart on one in particular.

I must have dozed a while because when Intha woke me up the sun was already low in the sky, gilding the odd cloud. Intha led the way back to the camp, the stench of elephant occasionally wafting back from him.

"Boss, do you think my girl is good-looking?" Intha asked after we passed beyond the river.

"Very," I replied honestly. "What did you say her name was?"

"It's Bua Kham."

I was still feeling drowsy and there wasn't much conversation until Intha struck an unexpected note.

"Boss?"

"What's the matter, Intha?" I asked gently.

"When we've worked out the forest, I won't go with you any more. I'm going to stay in Ko. I love Bua Kham." His voice was firm but as from afar. I thought back to the young girl I had just met on the riverbank. She was a little reedy in her blue blouse and ankle-length skirt but had a sweet face and nice round cheeks. After a pause, I asked, "What about Phlai Thong?"

He was silent and his drooping shoulders fell even further, indicating he needed some bucking up. "Well now, Intha, a man in love deserves some sympathy. It's going to take us at least another three years to work this area. After that you can decide whether you want to stick with me or stay here with Bua Kham. If you want to go on working, you can bring Bua Kham along. I'll see that you have your own hut separate from the others. It's a long time off; there's plenty of time to think it over."

His pocked face flushed, he stopped still and grabbed my arm, smiling brilliantly. A second later he was crestfallen again.

"I don't want to take Bua Kham into the camp. I hate those people."

"Which people?"

"The people in the camp."

I laughed off his fears. "If anyone messes around, I'll plug him." I patted the Colt automatic in the pocket of my trousers. Intha grinned.

"Boss, if anyone comes near Bua Kham, I'll bash his head in with this." He pulled his elephant pike from his belt and flourished it in the misty dark.

—2—

"Ten, twenty; two hundred."

"Ten, twenty; two hundred. Right."

"Eight, two hundred twenty."

"Eight, two hundred twenty. Right."

"Ten, three hundred thirty."

"Ten, three hundred thirty. Right."

The thumping of the marking hammers officially franking the logs so they could be hauled away punctuated the bawling out of the girth and length of the felled trees. From time to time a pungent curse would provoke peals of laughter.

"Pooped, Choet, really knocked out. Your whisky has put me right under," complained the big-boned forest inspector as he stretched himself lazily.

"Not sobered up yet?"

"What do you mean, 'sobered up'?" I'm dead beat."

"If all your sitting, eating, and sleeping has made you so tired, what would happen if you really did some work?" I was fed up after twenty days of extending hospitality to this town official by serving him whisky and eats in the shade of every tree he happened to be under. A dozen bottles of Mekong whisky would soon be finished. From the first day he came to the camp he proclaimed so that the whole forest could hear:

"Whisky, Mr. Choet, a forest inspector needs whisky. If he doesn't drink whisky, he's just a grass inspector."

The inspector's marking should have been finished ten days before, but what the hell, we should be grateful he didn't stretch it out for a full month. These law enforcement officials, conditioned by rules and regulations made to obscure responsibility, soon become petty tyrants to be approached by common people at their peril. It's rare to find a decent one.

"The job's done!" the workers shouted joyfully as the old boy waddled out from the shade of a thicket, me chasing him with the whisky. He glanced at his wristwatch and commented, "Exactly noon. Not bad at all."

Soon after lunch in the forest I returned to camp to find my friend alone, cheerfully plucking his mandolin.

"You have a good life," I said more severely than usual.

"The elephant's hot," he replied unconcerned, his hand still strumming.

"You're sure it's the elephant that's hot?"

He smiled and said nothing. When he detected my irritation, he added lamely, "The work is finished, boss."

After resting a while, I asked him, "Where's the elephant?"

"I let him loose on the path to Mae Hat Hill. What do you want me to do?"

"The inspector and his crew over there are going to leave."

I motioned to the three forest officers and a laborer sprawled on the row of logs set out under the shade of a tree in front of the camp.

"Intha, do me a favor and get them out of here. You'll be in Li before dark and can come back first thing tomorrow."

His silent gaze pleaded with me. His hands smoothed down his carefully dressed hair. When he saw I wouldn't relent, reluctantly he changed from his dark blue trousers into black cotton shorts, took off his sports shirt patterned with a map of the world and put on a dust-colored undershirt, tied a *phakhaoma*[1] around his waist, grabbed his elephant pike and left the camp house.

With the officials off my back, I wandered down to the beach of the Mae Ping River and proudly stepped along the logs laid out like a long raft along the bank. For us lumbermen, it was an incomparably satisfying scene.

We had staked our strength and lives to convert the teak trees from their stand on the high hills into placid log rafts of immense value, the trouble being that the "value" all went to people who have never seen a teak leaf. But that's the way it is here.

I got back to the camp as the sky began to blacken. When supper was over I lay down feeling rather tired and idly considered the fantasies about celestial forests in the legend of the Flying Swan being retold by an old man nearby.

---

1. A long, wide strip of cloth worn by men and used for a variety of purposes.

"Quiet, the inspector must be back," a worker signaled. "That's Intha's mandolin."

I strained to listen. The plucking sound was approaching, and in a moment Phlai Thong was there, swishing his trunk back and forth, in front of the hut.

"Why are you back?" I asked, vaguely.

"The officer told me to go away," Intha replied from up on the animal's neck.

"What happened?"

"When we got to Mai Wang village, they saw a man carting wood out of the forest and raised a stink. They pushed everyone back into the village and told me they were going to sweep the woods all the way to Li."

I headed off to bed paying little attention to Intha's clamor. "Here's a letter for the boss. The teacher in Mae Wang brought it in from the district town days ago."

—3—

The last few drops of the noon shower had fallen and the warm afternoon sunlight spread over the field in front of the District Office. The fresh colors of a misty rainbow arched across the eastern sky. I stumbled out of the district officer's house and swayed down the path under the veranda and then out on to the main road from Li to Toen. The refreshing breezes were chasing away the fluffy white mists still drifting among the trees and bushes. The green mountaintops overlay the azure horizon creating a dreamy atmosphere in Li but not for me. My anxiety over the district officer's well-meant joking was still ringing in my ears and the attitude of—well, my boss—was fresh in my memory.

"Look at Choet. He's been in the jungle so long his hair's turning gray. From the length of it, you'd think he was Tarzan," the district officer quipped as he nodded sympathetically in my direction.

"And what about Tarzan's girl? Must be a real honey. Tarzan always has the luck." He emphasized the word " luck" and screwed up his eyes with laughter

"Boy oh boy, prince, if you'd seen her would you be surprised," Phanit, the deputy district officer, joked before swallowing almost half a glass of whisky.

"Is that right, Choet?"

I only smiled. "Well, that's great." He shrugged his shoulders slightly. "So that's why he . . . er Choet won't come out of the jungle." When I didn't react, he forced a laugh.

"You've given it a try, have you, Phanit?" he asked turning to the young deputy.

"Well, I take the time to spend a night with Choet every time I'm in the Ko area on business, but those forest spirits seem to be a bit jealous," he bantered.

"Well, I bet you've already got some." He took another drink. "They say jungle love is hotter than a dry season forest fire."

The raucous ribbing intensified as the number of empty bottles under the table increased. I was fast getting drunk when a cool gust of wind blew in through the light green curtain reminding me there was an alternative to curling up under the table. Once outside, I walked unsteadily past Riu the Chinaman's shop, the police station, and the government's outpatient clinic down the Li-Toen road. A few civil servants and locals riding by on their bicycles smiled greetings, but the effect of the alcohol and my distaste of officialdom's style of partying made my own smile in return fairly wooden. Actually, I was disturbed from the moment I got the three-line note from our forest manager announcing the arrival of the nephew of the company owner and general manager and adding that he would be there to observe timber operations and might stay for the whole rainy season. As I was a simple commoner, my misgivings were multiplied when I learned that the nephew had the title of a minor royalty, a *Mom Ratchawong*. If he were a step higher in rank, you couldn't find a single person in the whole of Li who would know enough of the royal forms to talk to him. I was somewhat relieved when I noticed after his arrival that the tag on his suitcase gave only his name and address, with no indication of his blue blood, and thought this might indicate he wasn't too much of a snob.

Later that morning the boys brought the elephants to carry us back to Ko Forest. It was a tough trip: at times our elephants wallowed through the mud, sweeping it up in their trunks and blowing it over their backs. We were unrecognizably drenched and filthy. Past narrow paddy fields, crude houses clustered along the streams, we went through woods, gullies, and over scores of hills. It was tiring but there was satisfaction at seeing my guest excited and pleased throughout the trip. A number of times I had to smile apologetically when I could not point out to him the differences between certain kinds of trees he asked about.

"The bark of the *pao* tree is scaly with deep vertical cleavages and the leaves and trunk are lighter in color than the *ngae* tree." I rambled on about the differences as far as I could observe them, but after a time we came across a *ngae* tree with leaves and trunk lighter than the *pao*.

"Well, they all look the same to me," the visitor commented pleasantly.

Soon after our elephants crossed the teak line, we caught sight of the silvery Mae Ping River winding between the deep green hills.

"That's our camp, over there." I pointed to the distant huts ranged on a hill about five hundred yards from the river. The brown leaf roofs could be discerned among the tall trees. The guest from Bangkok looked at me and asked, "Why don't you stay with those people over there?" He pointed to the village of Ko strung out along the banks of the river lower down.

"We can't live with them, sir," I replied.

"Why not?"

"We have elephants," I explained. "Elephants uproot the villagers' banana trees and sugar cane. It's better to be where we are."

In a moment our elephant reached the landing between two of the camp huts. Intha strode out and smiled at us. Standing in the middle of the landing, he extended a sturdy arm to help me down and then did the same for the visitor.

"Have you stowed our things, Intha?"

"All done; I put yours in this house." He pointed to the hut on the right, which had been the laborers' dormitory. I had had it divided into two rooms, one for them and the other for me and fixed up the hut on the left for the newcomer.

"Ah, Intha, this is *Mom, Mom Ratchawong* Paipin Ratchaphruk, the nephew of our big boss. He's going to stay with us." I introduced the princeling hesitantly because I was uncertain whether Intha would understand the words I used, but I was relieved and pleased when Intha responded by putting his hands together in a very proper and respectful salute.

The honorable Paipin Ratchaphruk did nothing except to regard him interestedly. As Intha was leaving, he stared after him as if watching a freak.

"Funny, even has holes in his ears. 'Ear Holes,' that's a good name for him," the princeling commented vacantly as he followed me into his quarters.

I was walking back and forth watching several elephants tugging logs easily through the openings among the trees. Occasionally, when one would strike against a stump, the huge beast would stop a moment and scream. The rider and the foot mahout would both shout, "Hey, soke, soke," and the elephant would back up. "Peh, peh, peh—all right you're past it now, toh, toh," and, the obstacle circumvented, the elephant would forge ahead again as commanded. It was the last day we had to camp in the forest and a light shower invigorated both animals and workers. With the workable area getting further and further from the permanent camp, we had to spend fifteen long days in this deep wood with no possibility of getting back regularly to Ko, which all of us badly missed, especially Intha.

"Take it easy, there, tomorrow we'll be going back for certain," I cautioned as Phlai Thong dragged an enormous teak log right past me. Intha glanced at me a second and goaded the elephant on. I felt sorry for him. He had been brooding ever since we came in from the main camp two days ago, and nobody had the heart to tease him. On the contrary, we worked all the harder so we could go back to Ko as soon as possible. His love for Bua Kham was well known.

In both the camp and the village of Ko, everyone was cheering for them. If, any evening, Intha did not appear in the village astride Phlai Thong's neck swaying from side to side, plucking out the strains of well-known love songs, not only Bua Kham but many of the villagers would wait and ask one another, "Do you think it's Intha or Phlai Thong who's not well?" The next evening Intha would reappear happily playing his mandolin and replying with dignity to the worried inquiries of the villagers.

"The work area is a long way off—can't make it every night." I got pretty sentimental sometimes listening to him speak of his future. Coming back to the camp he would stop the elephant we were both riding on and in the clear tones of a happy man would point to a patch of thick forest on the long line of the hills and tell me, "Bua Kham and me, we're going to clear that land and I'm going to grow chilies, cucumbers, and rice."

During our trips, his eyes would roam among the trees and pursue his dreams, "Boss, help me remember that *pao* tree over there. I'll cut it down for the house."

That was the old Intha. His eyes that fixed me just a second ago were glazed. The trace of a smile in the corner of his mouth evoked the sadness of a lonely wood in the season of falling leaves. It was late; the forest and hills were sleeping in the chill mist. A few Karen mahouts were chatting softly around their fire under a low shelter. About twenty yards away Intha was sitting on a log picking glumly at his mandolin, the melody faltering. Unable to get to sleep, I got up and went outside and at the same moment Intha walked woodenly towards the hut.

"Your playing sounds awful today," I spoke out in the darkness. He stood still without answering and then followed me back to the same log. "Boss," he called softly while sitting down beside me.

"Boss, the man you call Mong, is he a Burmese?" Intha asked in dialect, confusing the title *Mom* with the local word for a Burmese.

"What Mong?" I asked bewildered.

"The man who's living at our camp."

I laughed. "That's no Burmese, Intha. He's a *Mom,* not a Mong."

"What's a *Mom?*" he persisted.

"That's what we call a prince or a lord. We can't address him like an ordinary person." I spoke very slowly.

"What kind of lord?" he interjected in a miserable voice.

I was taken aback. I knew how to answer his question without too much trouble but I sensed that the questions Intha was asking were a long way from what was really on his mind. I had lived with him long enough to know that he had absolute faith and trust in the lords he was familiar with: the lords of the forest, of the mountains, spirits in the trees, all the divine beings that regulated life and nature, but I was telling him about lords who were people and I doubted whether he would understand.

"Well, he's descended from a long line of lords, that is, he is a distant relative of our Lord of Life, Intha, whom we also call the Lord of the Land, the King."

He listened thoughtfully and then shook his head sadly.

"Boss, I don't understand. lord of what land? Where?"

"All of it, everywhere, Intha."

"You mean here and there?" he said pointing ahead and to the line of hills to the side.

"Yes, we pretend it belongs to him but in fact it doesn't really, but because he has great virtue and authority we hold him up as being the lord of all things. Ordinary people like you and me, Intha, are treated like his property and are called 'servants of the sky, slaves of the land' or 'subjects.'"

"You mean this sky, Boss?" he craned his pitted face up at the emptiness overhead.

"That's right, Intha. The prince with us is only a relative, a distant cousin, but still we respect him as a lord."

"Balls! Some lord! He's an ordinary man. I see him eat food every day."

I laughed at Intha's innocence.

"Who said he's not a man, Intha? The fact is he's just like you or me but he has certain things about him that it would be useless to try to explain. Where would a dope like you find the brains to understand?"

We were engulfed in strained silence. Still feeling superior, I tried to make out the reaction on his barely visible face, but it was he who broke the stillness with a question that numbed me.

"Boss, how is it that plain people can be lords?"

Were the starlight a little brighter, Intha would have seen my consternation. When I did not reply, he raised his voice to me, "Boss, you've gone mad. He's no different from us. To hell with lords."

"Mind your words, Intha," I warned him. "Don't forget, we're just ordinary people. Compared to him, we're only a speck of dust underfoot. You have to accept what everyone else does."

"Who's under somebody's foot—you or me?"

Before I could reply, he called me a fool and stalked into the hut.

With pity and disappointment, I watched his stocky figure disappear. What had happened to him? What could have transformed him so much? I went inside to bed without saying anything to him and fell asleep perplexed and discouraged.

—5—

"All finished, eh, Choet? You spent a long time off in the woods." The honorable Paipin Ratchaphruk greeted me cheerily as I passed in the shadow of the big shade tree.

"Yes, sir, it took a little while. The timber's a long way off. It had to be hauled out in two stages. I hope everything was all right for you here at the camp. I was worried about you, but the work never seemed to end."

"Quite all right. Everything here was just perfect. In a few minutes, Choet, let's have a drink together. These overcast skies seem to require it." He justified his invitation.

I laughed politely and went on to my room to change from my black working shirt into a faded native-style one, hung my blue jeans over a rail and put on green Chinese silk pajamas and went back down. The honorable Paipin in a tan watered silk T-shirt and a checkered sarong had draped himself on a log, a bottle of local whisky made palatable by the addition of a Burmese herb powder set next to him with a dish of sour fruits.

"The rawness goes out like magic with this stuff," he said as he handed me half a glass of whisky and a packet of the powder. "If it's not enough, I'll fill it up for you."

The sour fruit dipped in salt made the alcohol taste like sugar. We drank and chatted. His lordship advertised the diversions of big cities all over the world and I countered with puffed-up stories of life in the forest, repeatedly assuring him of my happy self-sufficiency over the years.

"Look over there, sir." I pointed to the crest of the hills on the other side of the Mae Ping River. "The white you see like diamonds strewn over green velvet is the line of teak trees in bloom. Have you ever seen anything more beautiful?"

He gazed and nodded his head in agreement.

"Even more beautiful at the foot of the hills are sylvan lilies, beautiful and ripe, calling out to be picked and savored." He flashed his white teeth in a laugh.

I put the glass down and asked him apprehensively, "Does that mean you've already found one, sir?"

"More than 'found,' old boy." He grinned, his red face complacent.

I took the next swallow of whisky without enthusiasm and prayed that his fine lily was no one I knew.

"Where did you meet her?"

"Right there in Ko village," he replied as he funneled some more red powder into the bottle. "Eh, what's her name again? Yeah, Bua Kham, that's it. You must know her."

It was like falling over a cliff. I was alarmed. My hands dropped to the log.

"I was waiting for you to come back," his voice continued to float towards me. "Tomorrow, have your men build me a little cabin down in the village on the bank of the river. Won't want to be up in the hills. Bringing her into the camp might disturb the others." He chuckled at the thought.

The clanking of heavy chains being hung on a railing nearby by a group of elephant drivers brought me to my senses. Among them was my friend and companion Intha, in a stupor like a sun-wilted bush, gazing in our direction, his eyes showing hurt and disappointment. Crushed, I walked over to the group.

Intha stood stolidly like a frontier marker. "I understand now, Intha. But we must always be friends."

He turned his back and went off.

I turned to his lordship, feeling sick.

"Excuse me, sir. I had something to say to the elephant boys," I mumbled as dusk settled into night. His pale arm lifted the red glass to drink, his only concern.

I told the boys to clear the bottles and the other junk and not to wait for me for supper. Then I left the camp and wandered down the hill leading to the village, the long grass beside the path undulating in the breeze blowing up from the river. I walked past the rafts of logs waiting to be released into the stream and threw myself down on the cool sand, disgusted and impotent. As with the rainstorm developing at the horizon, the moment of downpour could not be predicted. I lay there reflecting on myself, Intha, and *Mom Ratchawong* Paipin as individuals. Visibly we were all the same—men. But the invisible things—did they not make us unequal in human condition? I felt as I had before that I was standing at the point where sky and earth meet. It then struck me as peculiar that while we boast of being the most extraordinary of animals, with fine mental faculties able to vanquish all of nature, under the ground, in the heavens, we sometimes yield to such insubstantial things. You can understand how a man gets enslaved to position, property, and other intoxicants, but it is extraordinary when he bows down to spirits and other men he only imagines to have something special.

That evening I returned wearily to my room. It was quiet and still. I had not been sleeping long when I was shocked awake by an explosion of gunshots and commotion.

"What's going on? What the hell's happened?" I called as I rushed to my guest's quarters. "Has anything happened, sir?" I asked, dreading the answer.

"I don't know. It was big, round as a post, but soft and coarse. It moved across my chest and sprayed water all over my face," his voice trembled.

We shone our flashlights all around the room and found that a few hands of bananas set next to the bed were missing and the wall made of broad leaves had a hole as big as a man torn in it.

"Just an elephant, sir," I explained after sizing up the situation. "The elephant was just stealing some bananas. In feeling around with its trunk, it touched you, that's all."

As I returned to my house, I was startled to see, picked out by the waning moonlight, a pair of stocky legs hanging under the eaves, the rest of the form hidden in shadow. I recognized with a shiver that it was Intha and Phlai Thong.

—6—

"When are you leaving here, you bastard monkey," Intha shouted in Northern dialect while pounding the roof of the camp shelter with the back of his elephant pike and setting up a terrific racket. The workmen were aghast. *Mom Ratchawong* Paipin, his mouth hanging open, looked on drowsily.

"Intha!" I yelled. The elephant hook gleaming in the faint light of the early dawn remained upraised as if Intha were reflecting, and then slowly it came down.

"What's going on? What is that language he's shouting in?" the bewildered *Mom* Paipin asked me as I walked towards him.

"He made a mistake. He's mad because the elephant almost stepped on him and he thinks it was because you deliberately shot at his elephant last night," I covered up for Intha. Then I turned to get rid of the workmen.

"Go on, get on. What are you gawking around for? Get out. You too, Intha."

Intha didn't move.

"Intha, did you hear me?"

"Boss, . . ." He wanted to say something more but I cut him off.

"I told you to leave, Intha, I'll take care of this." Intha stalked defiantly towards the group of laborers.

"So that's all it is, just that trash beating on the roof at cockcrow," he grumbled as he went back to his room.

I filled my lungs with the damp cool air and drew my jacket around me. The atmosphere was depressing and tense. Some men had gathered on the log seat in front of the camp house, and apart from the sound of someone splitting kindling in the cookhouse, everything was quiet. Feeling dizzy and resigned as if I were riding a rutting elephant, I went to rinse my face at the end of the porch.

"I must be jinxed. First of all an elephant picks my pocket and now that silly Kamu boy with the holes in his ears almost knocked my roof in," the honorable Paipin jested as he stood with his arms folded across his chest by the bamboo rail slung with heavy chains. I tried to speak in a normal voice. "Sir, I think we're heading for trouble." He stared at me.

"Trouble?" What do you mean, Choet?"

"I mean for you and the way we all get along here at the camp, I mean . . ."

"You mean me!" he interrupted displeased. "I'm the one who's causing trouble, is that what you mean?"

"Yes," I replied firmly.

He heaved a long sigh. "Look, say exactly what you mean. I hate people who beat around the bush. What makes you say I'm the cause? You think I'm here to spy on you, to put on pressure . . ."

"No, not at all. All of us at the camp appreciate your friendliness; but I want to know the truth about Bua Kham."

The chill of the early morning haze seeped right to the bone. Paipin's aristocratic oval face slowly flushed. His hand that had been idly sliding over the chains stopped and he crossed his arms over his chest again. His frosty breath accentuated the resentment of his words: "You seem to begin to forget your place. I am *Mom Ratchawong* Paipin Ratchaphruk and not some worker you can pin blame on. You and everyone else here are under me. What I have to do with that bitch Bua Kham is my own private affair. Do you know what that means—'private affair'?"

I forced a smile. "Maybe, sir, you don't know that Bua Kham already has a man," I said in a voice I scarcely recognized.

"Oh, is that all it is, Choet? You said we were in trouble. I must apologize. I misunderstood. At first I thought you meant something else. Thanks for making the effort to let me know, but that sort of thing doesn't bother me."

"You've got it wrong," I said emphatically. "I mean, one of our men loves Bua Kham; they're really going to be married."

An explosion of laughter attracted the attention of nearby workers.

"For all your time in the woods, Choet, you still talk of love? Well now, you just tell whoever it is who's planning to get her—as long as it's not you—that he can just wait a little, because next month I'm leaving anyway."

I swallowed hard. "If I could have avoided it, I wouldn't have said anything to you, but if you saw how earnest the man is and how he's set everything aside for the girl, you'd realize there's human decency as well as love involved and would be as moved by it as I am."

My guest guffawed and asked, "Choet, how many years have you been in the jungle now?"

"Eight, sir."

"That explains it. You've been cut off from the world too long. You've become just like a native." He mumbled on as if to himself, "Love, human decency—it's all old hat."

He sat down pensively and then asked, "When you said 'one of our men,' who did you mean?"

"Intha."

"What! Human decency? You call that Ear Holes a human being like the others? Why he's just a Kamu."

The activity on the bank of the Mae Ping River was gradually obscured in the quiet darkening of evening until finally all was black. A light rain had started. Shouts and cheers from drunken festivities going on in the village erupted from time to time, not unlike the delighted croaking of frogs and things when the first floods come.

At the same time, in the quiet camp, some contrite workers hung around listlessly. Earlier, if they had had a little more sense, they wouldn't have to be ashamed of themselves now and Intha would not have disappeared. But they had no time to think. During the day, when the first man replied grudgingly, "I'll help you with the cabin, Your Highness," the others joined in one after the other, like waves lapping on the shore. Intha, their companion, suddenly got up, looked at them bitterly, and walked off like an old elephant into the forest.

"Stupid savage," Paipin smirked.

The sky was pitch black now. In a moment, it began to pour. Intha did not return. The storm carried the words "stupid savage" back into the minds of the remaining group of men with the question, "And what are we?"

Now, past midnight, the sky was still spilling over. Above the din of the storm, a few souls in the village of Ko heard a piercing cry and the call "Toh, toh" for urging an elephant to shove against a log. These sounds soon vanished with the rumblings of the end of the storm.

The warm sunlight of the new day illuminated the whole forest: the Mae Ping was running swift and overflowing. White mist floated higher and higher over the water and over the banks. The people of Ko, from the little children to the oldest, stood staring sadly at the bits and pieces of bamboo flooring and remains of the broad leaf roofing which the waters had pushed back up on the sandy beach.

"May she rest in peace. May both of them."

As the sun grew stronger, the crowd deserted the beach, but the sound of the river continued until the end of the rains.

1958

THE PLANK

กระดานไฟ

WHEN you leave the main road and walk upstream along the Lam Narai River for more than half a day, you come to three stunted trees marking the entrance to a narrow plain lying between precipitous mountain slopes on the one side and gravel hills on the other. The river at that point is no wider than the broad ditches that separate the raised strips of land in old orchards near Bangkok but it continues to flow with cool water throughout the dry season. On the hilly side of the river, the inhabitants had built a cluster of twenty-one houses; on the other side the rice fields extended to the foot of the mountain slopes. The village is called "Grandpa Yang's Plain," as if it were already a memorial to Yang Duangkhao, the old man who was the first to raise a home there.

He used to tell his neighbors that a fight with his father-in-law caused him to carry his wife away into the bush, but as he refused to say where he came from, some of the children of the second and third generations speculated that he was an outlaw who had fled from Lom Sak and others contended that he was a hunter from Chai Badan who, falling on this good spot, decided to settle here. His own nephews and nieces, claiming they had seen his bag of amulets and sacred objects containing several small images of the Buddha with Laotian features, favored the theory that he was a Lao from the Northeast. No one knew more. They knew far more about the crumbling stump of an ironwood tree in the middle of the village where the spirits dwelled.

When the children were very small, each time they passed the stump with their parents, they would see their elders raise their hands together in a sign of reverence. A little older, they were taught by their parents to put their hands together and make the same gesture. And it was not long before they were doing it alone. Later they taught their younger brothers and sisters to do the same. Each New Year's Day, one person from every family would gather there to make offerings and worship, appealing for peace and happiness, led in their petitions by the old man called by everyone "Father Yang" who ritually committed each newborn child in the village to the care of the Mother Spirit sheltered by the tree.

Khen's mother explained, "You, son, and also your mother, we owe our lives to the goodness of Mother Spirit who protects us. You see the axe marks on the stump." His mother pointed them out. "Father Yang chopped down this ironwood tree more than thirty years ago when, on arriving at this place, his wife was about to give birth to her first baby."

"What else does the Mother Spirit do for us?"

"So much, child. She saves us from sickness and fever, from the spirit that eats boys' livers, from the spirit that kills new babies, from the offal-eating night spirits that have light coming from their noses and from the forest spirits."

As the children matured, they learned of another sacred thing looming into their lives. And as their numbers grew, swollen by new migrants, the anticipation, awe, the terror of exclusion from this thing also increased.

The young man hurried down the path to the village headman's compound, not omitting to bow his head in respect to the dark stump near the front of the low house. When he looked up at the porch, he paled at the sight of a middle-aged man already in conversation with the old man. As soon as he reached the third step, the owner looked up at him and exclaimed, "Khen, you too?"

"Yes, Father."

The village elder sighed, his face troubled.

"Thit[1] Khieo has come for the same reason."

The young man sat down slowly, dumbfounded, mouthing words before speaking. "Father Yang," he spoke the village chief's name first, then turned to the older man whom out of respect he called "Uncle."

"Uncle Khieo, have a heart. It's my wife's first pregnancy. Your wife has had babies before. Please, please," he anxiously implored.

The man addressed, as "Uncle" remained silent, gazed at the sky and vaguely reflected, "Each to his own fate, Khen. Whether it's the first baby or the last, the risk of death is the same. It's up to a man's accumulated merit. The one who comes first, gets it; that's the way it's always been done. Isn't that so, Father?"

A call from a nearby house brought the distracted Thit Khieo to his feet. The young man stiffened as the old man, the pillar of the village, slowly rose and seriously, grimly, went into his house and came back carrying the stout, blackened plank that the people of Grandpa Yang Plain called "Holy Mother Ironwood."

The plank was about two cubits wide, a little more than two meters long, still rippled with axe marks, the ends covered with a thick residue of saffron and smelling of the forest-scented holy water.

A good while after the middle-aged man had carried the plank down from the house, the young man rose unsteadily and left

---

1. A title of respect for someone who has been a monk.

the house heading straight to the raised rice granary under which pigs used to be kept. The old man gazing after him was startled and cried out, "Khen, no, what are you doing? That's a plank from the floor of the pig pen."

Paying no attention, Khen dragged the plank from under the granary, perfunctorily dusted it, shouldered it, and walked off with his head high.

"I knew this would happen one day," the old man confided to the breeze from across the hills.

The thud of the plank falling from Khen's shoulder and knocking against a piece of firewood in front of his raised cottage attracted the attention of everyone then busy inside. Embarrassed, as he realized it was probably wrong to throw the plank down so unceremoniously, and avoiding the stares of several people on the porch, he bent down to take the plank into his arms as if in awe of it, and then took it behind the house to wash it with water from the big water jar. Then, in the fading light of dusk, he carried it up into the house to the fireplace.

His wife, face twisted with pain, was kneeling on the floor, arms upstretched gripping a long cloth tied to the roof-beam; two old midwives were bobbing up and down in front of her distended stomach.

"How's it going, Auntie?" he asked.

"It's almost time," one answered without looking at him. "Khen, did you get it?" implored his wife, in pain.

"Yes, I did. You won't die now," he reassured in a voice intended to be louder than usual.

The midwives looked at him approvingly.

"Then everything's ready?" the woman he called "Auntie" asked.

"Yes, the fire pot, firewood, hot water, black pepper, long peppers." He reeled off the items.

"And the blood tonic and the salt?"

"Not yet."

"Oh?"

"I have the salt, now. I have it." the voice came from behind.

"All right, but get the blood tonic ready," Auntie ordered.

"But what is it made of, Auntie?"

"Fire-threads and urine."

"What are fire-threads?"

"You dunce, you're about to be a father and you know nothing. They're the threads of soot that hang from the fringes of the grass thatch and bamboo webbing of the walls near the stove. Crush them fine and dissolve them in the urine and let her drink it."

Khen left the room.

The fire in the fire pot crackled while, from inside, came the sound of the pounding of the black pepper and long peppers in the stone mortar. Khen was sweating, the neighbors whispering. From time to time a moan floated from inside the room. He sat still, his mind jumping with thoughts laced with the fear of his deception with the lying-in plank.

"What's that sound?" Khen demanded as he made his way back into the room.

"Idiot, it was the cloth tearing," the midwife scolded him over the cries of an infant.

"What cloth? My baby's been born!" he exclaimed, his eyes fixed on the infant wriggling over the plank.

"Throw it on. Throw on some more." The sound of the large salt grains bouncing against the plank punctuated the midwife's orders.

"Does it sting?" the other asked repeatedly.

A moment later a weary voice answered, "It's stinging."

Khen, returning from the rice fields, hurried up the bank of the

Lam Narai, triumphant because today was the day his wife was to end her lying-in by the fire, and there had been no complications.

"It's about time people knew what's what. These stupid holy things," he commented to himself as he thought of the lying-in plank. He would proclaim to the whole village that it was all wrong, the belief they held since their father's time that any mother who did not lie by the fire after childbirth on the sacred plank with her baby would die an unnatural death. The "Holy Mother Ironwood" and the "Pig Sty Floor Board" were the same thing. Where does their sacred power come from? From men. But men's courage to face up to reason, that's what's sacred."

Khen's speech to the village for which he had already cleared his throat never came off. When he reached the threshold of his own house, the old man, head of the village, was carrying the plank down the step, both ends marked with saffron and both sides covered with ritual acacia leaves and candle wax drippings.

"Yes, Khen, Father Yang since this afternoon has been anointing the lying-in plank and did the ceremony of committing our child's soul. I gave him a baht for his services."

Khen laughed bitterly. "Look, dear, I don't care about a lousy baht but, believe me, sacred things don't make men what they are; men make them up to keep a hold over others."

Not understanding, she responded to his laugh with a little giggle.

1959

DUNGHILL

ฟ้าโปรด

AFTERNOON, late in the dry season. In a field dusted yellow by the waning sun, a few water buffalo calves occasionally bleated for their mothers. Once in a while their calls were returned. As on previous afternoons, Chom trudged after the buffaloes with the slow motion of an old man, waving a cloth to shoo his animals and those of his two grandchildren away from the rest of the village herd.

"Get a move on, Grandpa," the two kids taunted. "Can't you speed up? We're tired. We want to go home."

"Tired! From playing conkers the whole afternoon?" he snapped back. "I'm taking it easy for the buffaloes' sake. They're hot and tired. Water buffaloes are meant for water and where are they going to find it this season? You can't find a blade of grass that's not shriveled at midday. You watch them. Even when they're lying around in the shade, they wheeze like bellows. Farm boys should feel for their animals."

"Get off it, Grandpa. Tell us what you ate for lunch."

The white-haired old man squatted down on a low paddy-field wall, annoyed that the youngsters should remind him to be grateful to them.

"The bird we ate didn't fall from the sky by itself," the boy continued. "Lom and I chased it until it dropped. So did we, almost."

At the end of the afternoon, the few beasts culled from the herd were nibbling their way from withered grass blade to dry rice stalk, the two boys zigzagging after them looking for crickets. Calves caked with brown mud the color of the fields played along behind. The sun reddened as it touched the horizon. The children rounded up the animals and urged them on towards the hamlet. Chom remained on the dike swathed in cigarette smoke, gazing at the gray curtain of dust kicked up by the distant herd. Suddenly the kids' raucous squabbling brought him back to the scene. As he approached, each of the boys was indignantly stating his case.

"It was my buffalo. I saw it myself, it was mine."

"What's it all about? What's the fuss?" The old man was breathing heavily with the exertion of catching up with them.

The boys looked at each other and remained silent, but it took only a moment for Chom to guess the cause of the quarrel and when he did, his face fell.

"I saw it with my own eyes. It was my buffalo," Iang, the first boy, reiterated.

"Yeah, but it's my land and I won't give it up," Lom, the other, persisted as they both squatted down with their eyes fixed on the fresh mound of buffalo dung.

The old man ruminated on the problem for a time before pronouncing judgement.

"Now what do you say to this? The buffalo was Iang's and the field belongs to Lom. So we divide the cake, right?" he asked the first boy who averted his eyes and refused to reply. He turned to the other, "What about you, Lom? I'm asking you to divide it in half: half for you, half for Iang. Agreed?" Lom rubbed his stomach a few times and nodded instead of speaking.

"All right, Iang. Lom agrees. What do you say?"

"Okay!" The answer was firm.

The old man sighed with relief. "Good, now split it."

The boys' eyes met and they smiled as each broke off a twig to mark his portion.

"That's the way to do things. We live together, eat together, go hungry together, and when we do get something we share it. Tomorrow morning when the sun's up and the mists have cleared, we'll meet here and dig out the beetle grubs." When he finished, he invited the boys to drive the buffaloes on into the village.

"Why the face, Iang? Aren't you well?"

The boy said nothing.

The old man was concerned. "If you've got a stomachache, hold your breath, and chew a few of the new leaves over there, and in a second it'll be gone," he said, pointing to a bush.

"It's no ache; I'm just hungry."

Old Chom rested his hand on the shoulder of the boy and said softly, "Come on, let's get back home. You know, feeling hungry is just another kind of sickness."

The sun dropped below the earth, the sky turned gray, and a cool gust of wind blew from the north. The grandfather and the two children went in single file back to the village.

"Grandpa, did you say being hungry is just like being sick?"

"Yes, I did."

"Are there medicines and doctors for it then?"

The old man looked at the eyes of his grandchild and his faltering reply was lost in the rustling of the bamboo. The boy forgot what he asked when another cold sweep of wind made him hug his chest and scamper on ahead.

Before going off to sleep that night, Iang recounted the events of the afternoon to his mother and father. After the second run-through, his father commented acidly, "There wasn't any reason to go and divide with Lom. Not only was the buffalo ours, but you got to it first, didn't you? So why did you have to agree to divide it with him?"

"Well, I started running first, but Lom's legs are longer; he caught up with me and we got there at the same time."

"Never mind that. I'm sure that you *saw* it the minute our own buffalo dropped it . . ." the father's voice drifted off.

Poor Iang turned over and faced the wall feeling miserable. "I'm not sure, Dad. Lom could have seen it the same time as me 'cause we were walking together, and when I started to run, he came right after me. If he didn't trip, he would have got there before me."

In the dark, the boy heard his father sigh.

"Did you say you were supposed to meet him there when the sun's up and the mists have cleared?"

"Yes, Dad."

"That's fine. But don't you be a stupid fool. The buffalo's ours, so the dung's ours too. I'll get you up before dawn tomorrow and you go out there and dig out the beetles under it, hear me?"

Iang closed his eyes and imagined he saw a million succulent beetles as big as thumbnails swarming from everywhere in the world until they made the sky as black as themselves.

Lom's mother, a chill wind ruffling her fever-thinned hair, shoved her head under the eaves of the roof and reached out to shake her boy sleeping on the low porch.

"Lom, come, get up. It's already getting light."

He rubbed his eyes drowsily and noticed his mother's cool smile, which he returned conspiratorially. He threw his *phakhaoma* over his shoulders, came down the few steps, grabbed a hoe and an old pail.

The fog hung cold and heavy, and the old man's heart beat fast as he walked along by the thicket of bamboo. He was buffeted by greed, pity for the boys, shame at what he was about to do, and his conscience. As he turned the corner at the end of the grove, he stopped short and, through the fog, saw the two boys, each shouldering a hoe and carrying a pail, running towards each other from opposite directions.

"Lom! You dirty cheat."

"Iang, you're the cheat."

"Damn you, it's my buffalo."

"Stuff that. It's my field. If it's your buffalo, why don't you tell it to shit some place else."

"Go easy on that 'my field' stuff, Lommie. Your father's gone and pawned it. The time is about up; maybe he won't be able to pay and get it back."

"Fuck you, bring my father into it, will you?" Lom rammed his fist at his friend's eye. Iang ducked. Lom missed his footing and fell over on his head. Iang raised the handle of his hoe to full arm's length.

Old Chom was forced to intervene with a sharp shout. The boy stopped and turned to look.

An off-season rain began to fall. Iang and Lom drew apart and took shelter under the bamboo before running off to their homes to escape the rain. Then it dawned on them that their grandfather was also holding a hoe and a pail.

"Thank heaven for the rain," the old man reflected as he stood there shivering. "No dung beetles maybe, but at least we'll have shoots and sprouts for the boys to eat in a day or two."

1960

OWNERS OF PARADISE

สวรรยา

The Lord of all the deities, Indra, dwells in the second tier of Paradise, on the top of Mount Meru, 460,000 miles above the surface of the earth. The green god inhabits a palace with golden gates that are adorned with precious jewels and open to beautiful music. The divine creatures of this domain can assume any shape they choose; they can become as small as the end of a hair and feed on ambrosia.[1]

IN PARADISE

In the shade of a glowing day, in an ambrosial golden region, a pair of stem eyes blinked open.

"Hey, kid," cried a creature to the diminutive body of another as it slithered before him.

"And who are you to be calling me 'kid'?" was the answer.

"Are you addressing me?"

"Who else is there?"

"I'll tell you then, I own this place."

"Who, may I ask, taught you to be so proud of yourself?"

"Well, it's true."

"How come?"

1. A traditional Thai description of Paradise.

66

"The Prince of Angels himself ordained that I should be born in this abode of pleasure."

"That's a good one." A pause.

"If that's all you can say, it shows you're staggered by the truth." The second creature remained still as a third voice laughed, followed by a chorus of sniggers.

"What's going on? Who do you think you are?" the first retorted petulantly.

"The same as you," the newcomers jeered.

"You've got it wrong. You should be asking 'Who do you think *we* are?'"

"Look at yourself: see any difference between us?" The quarrelling tapered off and the thrumming music of an orchestra drifted down from above. "Well, any difference?"

"None."

"You saw none?"

"There's no difference at all."

The celestial harmony grew louder and in a moment the entire company ceased bickering and gazed upwards excitedly as the curtain of the sky was rent by the sharp green silhouette of the supreme deity in his appropriate color, flanked by his splendid attendants. He slowly descended in front of the group and asked, "O you heirs of accumulated merit, O you righteous ones, what is this commotion?"

"We have a great problem," the first volunteered.

"Speak."

"Initially, I addressed one of those here as 'kid,' which offended him, and when I informed him that I was the proprietor of this place by virtue of prior establishment, they all mocked me. In short, we cannot agree as to who we are."

"In our omniscience, we thought as much." The dignitary rubbed the palms of his hands together in thought and then continued. "All of you should appreciate that you are here as the beneficiaries of the righteousness of your ancestors."

"What does that mean?" they asked eagerly.

"Let us finish. All of you have come to this divine abode through the fruits of merit."

"Why divine?"

"We caution you not to interrupt us. This is the paradise of the righteous. All here is divine."

"If so, does that mean we are also divine?"

"If that is your understanding."

"Hey, ha, you're divine, we're divine," they bantered cheerfully.

"And who may you be?" a divine demanded.

"Do you really want to know?"

"Yes."

"If you were in the least observant, the luminescence of our person would have told you. Ah, but as you are newcomers, we will tell you. We are Indra, the lord of this habitation of bliss."

"O honored Lord Indra, forgive our simplicity."

As the divine host quieted, the surrounding attendants raised their voices and celestial music sounded. The newcomers entreated their lord to describe their Heavenly City.

"This world," Lord lndra intoned, "is coeval with the world of man and as for its location, starting from the sky, it is but two cubits to two fathoms lower than the surface of the earth. Everything, as you may see, looks as if it were made of gold, and as we are farther away, the sun's brilliance as it strikes the earth is filtered down to us in gentle rays and neither heat nor cold can reach us. Life is carefree and if we are hungry, delectable repasts from which to choose float down from the air. All, until the end, is felicity."

As these words ended, paeans reverberated through the heavens and the company of divines danced with joy.

ON EARTH

Late in the morning a man stepped out of the flimsy privy at the end of the field carrying an old tin still smelling of insecticide.

"Damn, more bloody flies every day. That should do it. Only the big green bastard got away."[2]

1962

---

2. This is an allegory which the author has never clarified. Since it was written toward the end of the absolute military dictatorship of Field Marshal Sarit, readers have been conjecturing about the symbolism of the green figure.

THE PEASANT
AND THE WHITE MAN

ชาวนาและนายห้าง

THE village is about twelve miles to the north of Bangkok. Its houses are strung along a canal each separated from the other by a water-filled ditch and a boundary of small trees. Most of them are low with *atap* roofs sloping down almost to the tamped earth beneath. The sleeping platform and kitchen are waist high and their wooden floors are wide enough to accommodate the family. Flower-patterned cotton hangings partition what space there is in the house. In front of each house there are either upended logs or a crudely made bench for friends to sit on when they stop by to chat. In the dry season the treadmill, rake, and plough are kept under the raised floor of the sleeping-room; the chickens roost there in the rainy season. Close by each house are a haystack and a buffalo shed.

The house, or more precisely, hut of Uncle Khong is not much different from the others. The absence, however, of a haystack and buffalo shed does not mean he is a special class of peasant who does not have to work for the name, only that at his age, no longer having the strength to wrestle with the soil, he superannuated himself.

The life of true peasants like Khong is uncomplicated, predetermined. When the rains come, they plough, then seed, then replant. If the rain is good, there's enough rice left over to sell, and if too much, they buy rice with what condiments, shrimp paste, and fish sauce they need on credit and wait to redeem themselves the following year. You can think of it as fate or call it, more flatteringly, as the townspeople do, heroism, and you would not be far wrong. Khong preferred to regard himself as heroic because, though he had not even a dot of land of his own, he was still able to provide for his wife and the many animals that depended on him as well as others provided for their families. If he had had children, he was sure he could do as well for them. In this vein, he boasted to Khem, his girlfriend, bride, and now old woman.

"If we had kids, I could do right by them, couldn't I, dear?"

"Yes, yes," she acknowledged, busy feeding all their six dogs. Never failing to give his pride a fillip, she added, "Even if we had six, they wouldn't eat more than this pack. That Somrit of yours alone eats more than the both of us together."

Khong glanced at the gangly puppy, legs spread, belly bloated, slurping rice gravy from a coconut shell. Being childless probably explained his fondness for animals. In his prime he kept the lot, from buffaloes to fighting cocks and fish. But as age advanced and energy declined, realizing he could no longer care for all, he sold them, even the farmer's indispensable buffalo. This did no great harm, though, for his work had already changed its character. Formerly his aim in growing rice was to earn enough to have extra money to spend and to donate at least as much as others to charity. Later he was satisfied if enough grew to feed his family for the year. As his capacity for heavy work ebbed, he took to gathering lotus flowers and leaves from the paddy-field ditches for sale to market vendors. This gave him enough for each day. Later, as he had an honest and grateful nature, the gentleman owner of the land he lived on was kind enough to ask him to oversee and collect rents from the newcomers. By then the buffalo was no longer needed. As Khong's eyesight grew poor and his hair turned gray, he could no longer defend his chickens from the wiles of the new generation of children and he gave up

71

trying to look after them. They were given away to whoever asked for them. Six dogs, four cats, and a few leftover hens remained.

Khong did not fancy the six equally; some he kept out of pity, but the one he really loved was "Old Somrit," the one his wife referred to. In fact, Somrit was only the spotted bitch's puppy and was born under the hut. His color was strange though, not mottled like his mother or dark like his father who Khong guessed was Blackie. Apart from his funny color, he differed from the other dogs in other ways: his ears stuck out and his eyes were small, like an elephant's.[1] The old man had thought that when he was a little older he would name him "Elephant." But he was called "Somrit" because of an event one day three months before. His landlord, when leading a group of multilingual foreigners in a boat along the canal, had stopped at his hut to exchange pleasantries and to give him another job—to show the paddy-field land and point out its boundaries to those interested. He willingly accepted. Just before leaving, the landlord noticed Somrit frolicking with a playmate in front of the house and exclaimed, "What an odd pup! You should call it "Somrit"—after all, it means bronze. That's his color." All the visitors agreed. When they left, Khong, feeling he loved the dog twice as much, clucked him over and patted his head, and from then on called him "Old Somrit."

The old man performed his new assignment enthusiastically. During those days, anyone passing down the canal who glanced at the bank would be apt to hear an old man in an old black shirt sitting together with his dog in the shade of a bamboo grove call

1. This description happens to be a stereotype of a late dictator of Thailand, back from treatment at Walter Reed Hospital in the United States, and in power when this story was written. There are similarities in the dog's name and idiosyncrasies such as a passion for cleanliness.

out, "Have you come to see my landlord's land?" Some said they had, others tittered, and occasionally the old man would laugh at himself for mistakenly addressing one of his own villagers. Those who did want to see the land were shown around with all the alacrity desired by the owner. Hearing new things in his talks with these people and walking side by side with persons he thought were millionaires made him happy. Occasionally a nice person would give him a cigarette and even offer to light it.

For several days Khong noticed a smallish boat punted upstream occupied sometimes by only one passenger, sometimes by several, which, as it approached his perch, would head into the thicket behind his hut. Though he thought they might be people coming to look at the land, to approach them would be inopportune. If they had come to see it, they would inevitably come to him for information. The boat would appear in the afternoon and remain until sunset. Sometimes the old man saw one of its passengers jump on to the bank—a big man in a gray shirt wearing a bell-shaped peasant's hat, looking up and looking down and finally disappearing into a clump of trees. At the beginning of the second week, the man could contain himself no longer and decided to take a look. With a snap of his fingers, he got Somrit moving and went along by the canal, the dog running ahead. When Somrit barked loudly, Khong quickened his pace and heard the dog being shooed away and then a greeting:

"How are you, Uncle?"

"Hello, eh?" He was surprised when the owner of the voice emerged from the bushes and turned out to be a tall white man with several large and small cases dangling from his shoulders, his broad smile evoking a grin from Khong.

"What are you doing there, sir?" he asked when he recovered from his confusion.

Instead of answering, the man pointed to the line of small trees

73

ahead of them, but seeing the old man perplexed, added, by way of explanation, "Birds."

"Ah, you've come bird-shooting," whispered Khong, spying a pair of bulbuls hopping along a branch. The white man shook his head negatively, his peasant's hat gyrating on his head.

"Not at all," he replied, peering through his binoculars. "I came to do research on birds."

Khong told Somrit to shut up and the foreigner handed the field glasses to Khong so he could take a look.

From then on, Khong so enjoyed going with his new white friend he almost forgot his landlord's assignment. The foreigner's manner was engaging and his angular body comical. Hunched over, his rump high, he bobbed along among the trees after a birdcall; it was not easy for Khong to smother a guffaw. And then, too, his bird-lover would bring him new and tasty snacks of which the soda pop was especially appealing. But the strongest reason for his affinity for the foreigner was the latter's show of affection for his dog Somrit. When his bird watching was over, he would call Somrit over, rub his back, and give him a big biscuit. The triple friendship grew daily. The old man of Bang Jak canal sometimes invited his new friend to visit his hut but there always seemed to be some obstacle.

Late afternoon one day after the passage of almost a week, the white man told him that the birds they had been observing with fascination had laid some eggs and he would be back in five days or so to see them, but in the meantime he would ask Khong to keep the local boys from disturbing them which Khong willingly agreed to do. Finally, he asked about Somrit who did not accompany them that day. Khong replied that Somrit was sick from the previous day, having so overstuffed himself with food he couldn't get up. At this, the foreigner opened his eyes wide and questioned, "What did you say is wrong with him?"

"Overeating. His belly's so full, he can't get on his feet."

Reflecting for a moment, the white man asked, "Can I visit him?"

"Please do."

The foreigner smiled at Khong's eagerness.

Khong guided his important guest along the path beside the narrow waterway to his hut and called out to his wife, Khem, "Khem dear, the foreigner has come to visit us."

The old man called again and again but there was no answer except for the initial howling of the dogs, which he stopped with a sharp word. His composure lost, he mumbled apologetically, "Not in."

"Who's not in?"

"My wife. Her name is Khem."

The white man laughed. "That's all right. I came to visit Somrit."

"Where's Somrit gone, Khong?"

"It's you, is it, Mr. Yot?" Khong peered at his friend, the schoolteacher, sitting under the canopy of the small boat.

"He was sick so the foreigner took him to the city for treatment. Where are you going in that boat?"

"I'm just getting a ride to school."

Every morning Khong would sit comfortably at the bank of the canal under the bamboo in front of his house. In the afternoon he would walk along the bank turning into the path along the ditch towards the line of small trees where he would busy himself until evening watching the antics of his pair of birds hopping and flying about the trees now festooned with yellow flowers. It became quite pleasant. Sometimes he would try to imitate the birdcalls and would catch himself chirping and peeping even after the birds had disappeared into the shrubs. They have just a few words, he reflected, and manage to get on together whereas men have thousands of words but still can't hit it off.

On returning after dark one day, he replied to his wife's inquiry after Somrit, "Not yet. The white man hasn't come yet but the birds are still there singing in the evening."

Khem smiled and shook her head at Khong's comments, which would usually include the white man and the birds.

"What about Old Somrit? You said the foreigner would bring him back in five or six days."

"Take it easy. Tomorrow or the day after. How do we know how sick he was? The white man said he had to be taken to a doctor. What a lucky dog he is," Khong said emphatically.

The following day, the foreigner did come, but without Somrit. He said that he had sent him to a training school.

Astonished, Khong could only exclaim, "What? A dog school!"

"That's right," the big white man said.

"What in the world do they teach them to be?"

"They teach them to be as clever as people," the white man continued when he saw Khong appear uneasy.

"They'll teach him to know his duties, to guard the house, carry things for his master, catch thieves, and also to be clean and not to make messes." The explanation was lengthy.

"Can they do that?"

"Absolutely," the foreigner asserted.

That evening the villagers traveling along the canal in front of the hut heard the voice of the old man chatting interrupted by the sound of thin laughter from his wife. Thinking it over, Khong decided he had come upon one of the wonders of the world.

"Listen dear, city dogs can do anything. That's why they're so expensive; they cost even more than a full-grown working buffalo. If it weren't our white gentleman who said so, I wouldn't believe it."

Finally, the day awaited by both husband and wife came, but Khong was badly disappointed to see Somrit whining in the boat, refusing to get out. When at last they got him on to the bank, he snarled at the old man and struggled to get back into the boat. Embarrassed, the white man threw a biscuit to the dog and pushed off leaving him whimpering on the bank. Khong and Khem exchanged glances.

"Looks like he's forgotten the taste of rice and gravy." The woman spoke first.

"It looks that way," the old man said regretfully looking at the dog biscuit with misgiving.

After he had gulped down his special food, Somrit leaped at one of the hens, snapping at it around the house, and when it finally escaped by flying on to the roof, Somrit turned on one of his old friends who was wagging its tail to welcome him back, seized him by the throat and flung him around. Unable to stand it any more, the old lady seized a paddle and slapped it sharply down in the middle of Somrit's back. Somrit, squealing, slinked off under the house.

"Look at that. You eat a few fancy meals and think you're a big foreigner. I'll break your back with this paddle in a minute," she threatened the dog again.

"Lay off him, Khem. He's just back from good food and good times over there. Let him show off a little. When the smell of the white man wears off, he'll be himself again."

"Foreigners, bah!" The old lady leaned the paddle against the house-post. "You just watch. He's not yet finished with this foreigner business. Here we were counting the days to his return, and when he sees us he growls in our face."

"Well, if he knew what was right, he'd be a man not a dog." The old man continued to take the dog's part and his wife walked away petulantly.

The following morning Somrit was no better. He was moping, refused to eat, gave a nasty look at anyone that came near, snarled, and growled. At noon the teacher, Yot, paddled up to the front of the house and called out, "Has Somrit come back? I thought I heard him bark."

"It's awful, Yot," the old man complained as he walked out to the landing.

"Since he came back from the city, he's refused to eat rice, behaves so proud, and goes after the other dogs."

"But you said he'd been sent to a training school."

"Yeah, I don't know what they taught him. He's been ruined."

The teacher mulled over the problem and advised, "Maybe he just feels a little strange in these surroundings or he's learned new habits. I hear at these dog schools they train dogs to love cleanliness, to relieve themselves in the proper places and not to accept food from strangers so as to avoid poisoning." The teacher expatiated in the manner of people who feel they know a great deal. Finally, he asked Khong, "What did you put his rice in?"

"A coconut shell."

"That will never do," the teacher was quite positive. "You can't treat him in the old way any more. Try putting it on a plate."

The old man disappeared compliantly into the kitchen and emerged a moment later with an enameled dish full of rice mixed with fish.

"Somrit, here, Somrit."

The dog emerged from under the house, sniffed at the plate put down in front of him, and proceeded to lap up the contents.

"What did I tell you?" the teacher remarked smugly. "These trained dogs are very particular about cleanliness."

Somrit, finished eating, turned to bark at Khong.

"Now, what's bothering him?" the man asked

Yot thought for a moment, then instructed Khong, "Ah, I know. Put on your best clothes."

"What?"

"Don't be stubborn. Play along with him."

Khong went inside to change into a new pair of black pajama

trousers, a faded blue shirt, wound a red *phakhaoma* around his waist like a sash and put on a palm leaf farmer's hat.

"How's that?" he asked as he appeared from under the roof. The teacher pointed to the hat and motioned him to remove it.

"It makes you look too much like a peasant."

The man obeyed and strutted into the center of the yard, standing there elegantly.

"Somrit!" He snapped his fingers to call the dog over. The dog wagged his tail a little but in a moment started to bark again.

"Damn!"

"Not fine enough, Khong."

Khong cocked his head to one side and murmured, "Just like a teacher to know everything." Then he spoke to the dog, "I know what you're after, my Somrit. To please you I'd like to put your food on a golden plate. But what to do? As for my clothes, these are the only good ones I have."

Before he finished, Somrit raced to the boat landing, whimpering happily. When Khong and the teacher, squinting against the sun, recognized the landlord, Khong followed and raising his hands in respectful greeting said, "You've come early today, sir."

"How are you? Everything all right?"

"Yes, sir."

"Well, I see Old Somrit has grown a lot," he said, changing the subject when he noticed the young dog making a fuss on the bank.

Khong sighed deeply when he saw two foreigners sitting in the boat also eyeing Somrit.

"Hello, doggie," one of them called out.

Somrit increased his whining.

The landlord said nothing more except to tell the boatman to move on. When the boat was gone, Khong walked over to Somrit. "Henlo, henlo," he said trying to imitate the greeting of the foreigner. He bent down to hug the dog, but the instant he stroked the dog's back, Somrit dug his teeth into Khong's shoulder. Khong grabbed a stick and brought it down hard on Somrit's head. Before Khong could strike again, the squealing dog scurried under the house. "Bite your own father, will you?" His voice trembled with anger. The commotion brought Khem and Yot hurrying over. When Khong pointed to the wound in his shoulder, they looked at each other and were stunned but the teacher, as usual, recovered quickly. "He was just doing what he thought would please his trainers."

"What should I do with the animal?" Khong wondered as he walked into the hut.

"Why ask? It's your dog, Granddad. You brought him up. You can do what you like with him." The teacher got back into the boat. The old man went into the house, set a pillow against one of the posts, and settled down against it, closing his eyes, his mind wandering off into the paddy fields. A furious barking roused him. About ten people were standing in front of the hut.

"Khong, I've agreed to sell this land to these people. They're going to put up a factory. It's all right for you to stay on. You needn't move until they begin to build."

Khong assented respectfully. His eyes swept around his house, and he thought of the factory, the chimneys. His shoulder throbbed. He thought of the teacher's words, "You brought him up . . ."

1966

CLASH

อุบัติโหด

SURE, I know you can't go through life without depending on other people but I never thought that you had to be grateful to anybody else for dying. Especially my own death. I could never imagine any reason why I should have to thank anyone for that—that is, until it happened. That night I knew I was deeply indebted to a person I never met and whose name I could hardly recall.

People often talk of premonitions, even more after the event, especially where death is concerned. I thought about the events of the previous day and even the days before that, but I could recall nothing that could possibly have indicated that I was due to die. There was maybe one thing but I wouldn't really consider it an omen. On the very day, I was having a cup of coffee in a coffee shop when a fat-faced, round-eyed, balding fellow sat down at my table. He was a life insurance salesman who seemed to be impressed by his own sales ability. Engagingly combining the cunning of a wild boar with the smoothness of a professional speaker, he harped on my death and tried to depress me with visions of my family suffering if I didn't take out insurance with his company. But if you treat a sales talk by an insurance broker as an omen of impending death, I would have been dead long ago. As always, however, his mystical string of statistics overwhelmed me, but after a while I grew tired of meekly agreeing with everything he said and finally a friend at the next table interrupted his performance.

"That's all very well," my friend said, "but how come the insurance companies all seem to die before the clients?" He had hit a sore spot. The salesman, defeated at last, got up and walked away.

I left the shop and drove past the movie house on the way to the market. A crowd had gathered in front of the billboard that announced the current film. I remembered it was a Japanese movie about a samurai swordsman. I'd been wanting to see it ever since I saw a poster about it in the coffee shop the month before. I made a quick stop, parked, and bought a ticket. It was a good picture, so I wasn't sorry that I spent the money. I was carried away by the hero, an intrepid and devoted knight who wound up in the middle of a highway in his death throes.

I was hungry after the show, so I stopped at a food stall, but before I'd had a chance to order, a friend sitting in the stall with his mouth full motioned towards my car. "The ambassadors' ladies are circling your car," he said. "Perhaps their ladyships want you to drive them some place?"

I laughed and the others smiled as we glanced at the two girls standing in the shade of a tree. They were both dressed for work in red miniskirts starting below their navels with the hems well above their knees. Flimsy knitted nightie-like tops barely covered black brassieres. My friend, still joking, made signs at them and pointed to me, I suppose to show I was the driver of the unlicensed taxi. I had not yet made up my mind about what to do when suddenly both of them came straight over to me.

On my way back from the new market outside the town near our ally's military base where I dropped the girls, I mulled over the expression my friend had used—"ambassadors' ladies"—which had caused the people at the food stall to smile. I wondered if other languages had phrases for them as vivid, derisive, and nicely sarcastic. Who had invented this nickname for camp-following floozies? Had he been more revolted by the rented wives or by the foreign soldiers who, with the immunity of diplomats, swarmed over the brothels and massage parlors?

Perhaps having the whores in the car had hexed it. But surely not—it wasn't the first time those ladies had ridden with me. I have nothing against them, and anyway I don't believe that nonsense. They can give you the clap, that I believe. But then, if you're not careful, even good expensive food can make you sick. If it's true that prostitutes bring misfortune to mankind, there would be nothing much left in the world. It would be the end of limousines, buses, trains, and planes in the air, not to mention unlicensed taxis. From the smallest roadside food stall to the fanciest restaurant with entertainers and singers, from the shops selling diamonds to those selling lavatory brushes, from the makeshift offices of the county headmen to the great government offices, is there any place that has not known their presence?

When the afternoon sun began to barbecue the road, I went home to take a lazy nap. Later, I was awakened by the radio next door announcing the results of the week's lottery. I splashed water on my face and drove to the bus station. I parked and went into my regular coffee shop where some friends had already gathered. They kidded me for being late and asked if I had bought any lottery tickets. I told them I had got some with different end numbers and ordered a coffee while we listened to the results of the draw. I could have listened in comfort at home but it wasn't as much fun as listening at the coffee shop. We weren't really concerned about the winning numbers and no one thought about checking the tickets, which were still in our pockets. We were more interested in betting right there and then on the last figure of the first, second, and third prize numbers.

On some of these occasions, if enough people were game, bets were placed on the second or third figures. As usual I liked to hang around the coffee shop on lottery day and didn't leave until after dark. The fun over, I felt exhausted and regretted having lost money.

On my way into the busy, well-lit bus station I saw a monk who looked familiar standing quietly by himself and asked him where he was going. I wasn't out to make money off a monk. I thought that if he was going to a place nearby or if he lived along the road to my house, I could do him a good turn and gain a little merit in the process, but when he named a distant town, however, I forgot the merit business. I got into the car and was about to take off when three men hurried out of the bus station and asked how much it would be to hire the car. I answered offhand, a hundred and fifty baht; it was twice the regular fare. Without hesitation, which seemed odd, they opened the door and all three got it. And as the monk was going in the same direction, a little beyond their destination, I asked permission to take him along. They said it would be all right, so I backed up, opened the door, and invited the monk into the car. At first he was bewildered but then murmured a blessing and climbed in.

We reached the outskirts of town and I realized how late it was when I saw the thin crescent moon shining dully above the treetops. The road, though it wound through hills for a short distance, presented no problem for I knew it like the palm of my hand. It had been built a little over two years before and was the best road modern equipment could make with every curve and every bridgehead carrying reflecting traffic signs. I can never recall the official name because everyone calls it the "Progress Road," just as the villages along both sides of the road are "Progress Villages," each displaying a big name-sign in Thai and English. I was sailing along in good spirits, amused that, as lazy and indifferent to work as I had been that day, I was making all of a hundred and fifty baht and earning merit as well by giving a free ride to a monk.

We were over a hill. Beyond the next curve, we would be on the level plain scattered with villages. I slowed down for the curve and accelerated again on the straight. At that moment the monk, whom I thought was asleep, yelled. Two water buffaloes, one chasing the other, lunged out of the bushes onto the road. As I swerved to the opposite side, my headlights picked out the rear end of a dead lorry in the dark. It was too close to brake. I spun the wheel and smashed with a terrific noise into a bridge railing. The door must have come off because I felt I was being whirled into the air. Then I was aware of being on a raised path by a paddy field. I could make out cries of pain, moans, calls for help, but little by little they became hoarse and faded away.

So there I was in a very bad accident. It could not have been avoided. An angel (if there is such a thing) could have been in the driver's seat and still it would have happened. I was completely stunned. I couldn't help myself, much less the others. Suddenly I was aware of people running and I could see them shining their flashlights about. Four or five men snatched up the things that lay scattered around the car. On the other side of the wreck, the moans began again. The men moved toward the sounds.

"This one's not dead yet," someone said. Then there was the klunk of something hard, like a lump of earth or rock, striking twice on a skull. I could almost see what was happening. The death throes of the samurai swordsman in the movie I had seen at noon told me in a flash what to do. I turned my face up and held my breath. My mouth hung open, eyes rolled up and frozen fingers seemed to clutch at the air. Just in time. Two shadows approached and loomed above my head. They yanked the watch from my wrist and a sharp pain creased my neck when they tore off my gold chain. A voice from the edge of the road called out softly, "Someone's coming." The group loped off into the dark.

I took a deep breath and looked. I could make out the lights of a number of small storm lanterns approaching. Several in this band were carrying hoes, knives, and sticks as if set to catch frogs during the rice-planting season. One man raised a lantern high over his head near the car. "Cripes, a monk!" He lowered the light. "There's a monk stuck in the car. It looks like . . ."

After a moment of silence a voice replied, "Yeah, he was a rich one. Where's his bag?" I could hear the car door being pried open with a terrific racket. With that, remembering my swordsman, Toshiro, I set about dying for the second time and tried to do it better than the first. I closed my eyes and gaped with my lips pulled back. Now, however, my fingers were held straight to make it easy for them to get my ring off. I realized that in my first attempt at the role, when my curled fingers interfered with the removal of my watch, I had probably just missed having my hand chopped off. Besides, for me to die with my fingers clenched was unlikely as I was supposed to be dying on a sultry evening in the dry season. When the samurai died, he was on a highway freezing in a heavy snowstorm.

The group began their frenzied search for the corpses' belongings but soon lost their enthusiasm and began speculating in whispers on the cause of the accident and on luck and fate. Some of them sympathized with the victims; others thought they got what they deserved and the men finished by comparing the violence of this accident with the last. The braking sound of an approaching car broke off the conversation. A villager replied to an inquiry from the driver. The engine stopped.

"Police, police," they passed the word along softly.

I tried to raise myself but could not. My whole body was in

pain and I thought something must be broken. A police officer swept his light among the bodies. "Hey Sergeant, take a look at this one! It looks like him."

The sergeant and the others examined one of my passengers. After some hesitation, another voice confirmed the first opinion. "Yes, that's him alright, that's the Tiger. Not much to be afraid of now."

"Now that we've got him, do we get the reward?"

"Sure, if we show we cornered him."

"Hell, that's easy, I'll put a hole through his head, all their heads."

It was quiet again. This time I did not think of the samurai but concentrated on the image of Buddha and began praying.

"Don't be a fool!" the first voice that had called over the sergeant broke the silence crossly. The policemen then lackadaisically inspected the scene. I could make out only that they were talking about a group of bandits. "How many were there, exactly?"

"The guy they held up said six."

"Then one is missing. And when did the monk join the gang?"

It was the first time I ever felt ashamed of being a member of mankind and I wanted to cry.

Dogs barked and bayed. By then all the villagers must have known what had happened. Doors opened and closed as people stopped their cars and got out to look. From the transistor radios carried by the villagers milling around, I heard reedy country songs and a sermon on the message of the Lord Buddha.

1969

DARK GLASSES

แขมคำ

MORE familiar than an ordinary visitor, though known about rather than seen, it often walked on invisible legs into the mother's heart and left again, as featureless as before. It came and went but she did not know how. Sometimes it came after midnight; sometimes it intruded in the early morning and lingered until nightfall. It followed her into the rice fields and stayed with her as she gathered leaves and sticks for the fire. It didn't visit just anyone, only people well known to it like her and the father.

A few days before, while she was busy preparing for the temple festival, it vanished, and she could not recall exactly when it came again or where it came from. She had been stitching up a new sarong for Bunpheng, her youngest son, when from the wood a gong boomed. She put her work down and looked over the fields where no breeze, no cloud in the azure sky, disturbed the soft afternoon sunlight. The gentle but sad reverberations saturated the landscape. She turned her eyes back to the blankness around her. Bunpheng's blanket was still heaped on the mattress on the porch where he slept; beyond it, the plaited bamboo partition of their room—hers and her husband's—and next to it was the solid room, properly walled with wooden boards, its door shut, empty. She stared at it for a long time. It was probably then that it welled into her heart again, this anguish.

Any living thing nearby would have dispelled the anguish, a

little lizard on the roof-beam, a wasp on its regular flight past her head, but they were not there. The yellow sparrow that used to cling to the tree in front of the house was gone. Its absence reminded her of another bird she had ignored in a cage hanging from the eaves. The sight of it made her feel good and as she approached, the still creature fluffed its wings, stretched its neck, and cooed. Unaware of the warm tears in her eyes, the mother glanced over to the sealed door in deep shadow. The father often stood there motionless for so long she wondered what was wrong, but never, until now, did she realize why.

It was hard to believe that three years had passed since the very day of this annual festival. Well, perhaps, not the very day. In fact it all began several months before this season on a bright afternoon soon after the harvest. She and her husband returned early to find a car parked under the mango tree in front of their house, the same one that more than once had passed by in a cloud of sand-dust, not that she had seen it clearly through the billowing obscurity. It was something new for the villagers of Dong Khaem and the mother knew like everyone else from gossip that it was the engineer's car. She did not know when those people had appeared although from their conversation with her daughter, she thought it could not have been long before. The father had gone straight up into the house while the mother fussed with some mangoes and kept an eye on her daughter who was sitting at a loom weaving. The two men around her daughter, both wearing wide-brimmed hats and light blue long-sleeved shirts, were smiling conspiratorially at one another. Whether or not they saw her too, the mother could not tell because of the dark glasses both were wearing.

"You were born a beauty, Khaemkham," the one leaning on the loom said.

"Born a real beauty, Khaemkham," the friend of the first echoed.

The mother couldn't make up her mind whether it was better to stay or to go up into the house.

Khaemkham, in whose dialect the word for "beautiful" merely meant a time of day, replied, "Oh no, I was born in the afternoon."

"Is that so? Well, still born beautiful."

"No, you don't understand." She rested the purple-threaded shuttle on the cloth, brushed her hair away, and looked at the dark glasses.

"Why don't you listen to me? I was born in the afternoon."

The young men's eyes exchanged smiles and the young girl continued.

"My mother told me that when I was inside her, she began to have labor pains while she was harvesting rice in the fields and my father brought her back to the house and I was born in the afternoon. Isn't that right, Mama?"

The woman was startled to be called as a witness by her daughter.

"That's right, Khaemkham," her mother's voice was unsteady, "Khaemkham was born in the afternoon, later than it is now."

As she spoke, she measured the height of the sun now touching the tips of the trees, but before she could continue the father interrupted from up on the house.

"Dummies, both of you, mother and daughter. They were just saying, in Thai, that she's pretty."

The tone of the father's voice was short and not pleased. At supper the mother saw her husband look at their daughter as if he wanted to tell her something but it never came out. There was no moon that night. The father sat alone at the end of the porch and did not go in to sleep until after midnight, and in the room with walls of proper boards the mother heard Khaemkham turn and twist restlessly until the same late hour.

The mother knew as did the rest of the village that the father treasured his daughter for a deeper reason than that she was the only one. Before the mother had moved into the village of Dong Khaem, her husband had migrated with her in tow from place to place so often that she became inured to it, but when they reached Dong Khaem, the father declared they would not move again and he set out to clear fields for growing rice.

Delighted when Khaemkham was born the following year, he named her himself, which he had never done before with the other children, and when the newborn child turned out to be a weakling, he blamed himself for working his wife too hard. So concerned was he to save Khaemkham from heavy work that his neighbors, and especially the country lads, made fun of him. As their house stood isolated at the edge of the paddy fields, the father was meticulous in fencing it. One day the local boys, who would take delight in taunting him from outside the fence, called out, "Hey, it's thorns that make a fence, Uncle, not the smooth bamboo you used!" Though not a man open to suggestions, the next day he went out into the wood to dig up some spiky bamboo to add to the fence. The road that was built opened up not merely backwoods villages but the fences and doors of the villagers' homes. The father fell victim to further adolescent teasing. "Spiky bamboo can keep out water buffalo and farm boys, all right, but it's not much good against cars."

The father's uneasiness came with the passing of the rain clouds from the sky. Dong Khaem ceased to be a remote hamlet. The villagers, excited with the new road, took to gathering under the eaves of the coffee shop and began to go around more. The young people, the girls and boys, got kicks by hitching rides in the construction trucks even as far as the district town. They returned dressed in gaudy clothes from the market. But the father went more often to the temple, and became more reserved. "I'd put it off, if possible." He was speaking of the merit-making festival held every year in the fourth month. "If no one's interested any more, why should I worry." But he was wrong. Before long, the people got used to the new things, to the strangers and then to traffic on the road, and turned their talk to the festival although it was not quite the same. This time it began with green and red invitation cards printed in the town and handed out to all the families and even to people living outside the village.

On the night of the festival, the temple, which used to be all rosy and warm in the light of torches and incense, was now brashly lit by electric light supplied by a portable generator and strident with people and music. The pulpit that used to be so fresh in a mantle of banana leaves, sugar cane, and wild flowers was now festooned with flashy multicolored cellophane. Cars, trucks, and buses squeezed into the temple yard. The monk's sermon, blasted forth by loudspeakers, could be heard in several surrounding villages.

The mother's wandering mind returned to her sewing for a moment and then again sought out the birdcage.

It had bright red little eyes. Each time the mother moved, it bobbled its head and cooed. The big gong tolled again but though its voice was as soft as before, the loneliness of the sound had vanished. She glanced from the birdcage out across the rice fields to a cluster of figures moving out of the trees beyond. The sound of the gong became more frequent and was punctuated by periodic cheers from the procession. As it neared, she could see the old monk, composed, on the palanquin moving forward in the front. Then she could make out the fluttering ends of the pink and green sashes that would be Kanha and Chali, the children of Vessandara, the Buddha-to-be. Behind them were the villagers, some carrying flowers and leafy branches from the forest. Her husband was carrying the gong at the rear of the file. She gazed after it until it turned and disappeared around the bend at the end of the village. A little later she heard the deep thrumming of the temple drum telling the world Vessandara had come home. Then would be the time to decorate the pulpit with the branches, flowers, and leaves.

The mother could not remember when the little bird came to share their roof. She guessed it must have been when she was so upset she didn't know whether the moon was waxing or waning and her husband had withdrawn into stunned silence. When her grief had abated, she noticed him fooling with the birdcage but never felt like asking him about it. This was really the first day she had taken a close look at the bird, a pretty thing looking as if it were sculpted out of perfumed talc. As she came to love the tiny bird, understanding of her husband and sorrow at thinking him heartless for his outward indifference to the disappearance of their daughter as if she were but a calf suffused her heart. After that Vessandara festival years before she did not think her husband would go again to the temple and she never thought she would again see such a fine procession as had just passed. The fields were still bright, the air getting chilly, and she realized that grief, no matter how great, in time and if life lasts, relents.

The father returned home before the sun had disappeared, and though weary, his face showed contentment after the merit-making ceremonies. He was holding a little box of saffron and hesitated a bit when he saw his wife standing next to the birdcage.

"It's a tame little thing," he said as if not knowing what better to say.

"It is."

"I didn't mean to keep it caged so long. You know, I thought when its wings were strong enough, I'd let it go. Well, three years have already slipped by. I've made it suffer enough. What a shame."

"Yes," was all the mother could say.

Early the following morning, after blowing saffron water on

the bird for good luck, the father carried the cage to the temple and, at peace with himself, listened to the sermon. When the gong sounded the end of the chapters it was almost noon; he prostrated himself three times in the direction of the monk and then crept over to the cage placed at the foot of the pulpit. On seeing the man, the bird cooed softly to him. He smiled with joy. His neighbor tittered.

He turned to his wife. "Join me in letting the bird go?"

"You go ahead."

"Well, it's really my sin to have kept it locked up."

The father carried the cage from the temple, passed under the sacred bodhi tree, and cut across the field to the end of the fence where he put the cage on the ground. A few children trailed after him to watch. "Let this be the end of our troubles," he intoned. He extended his hand to the door of the cage. "Back to the woods, little bird. Help your mate hatch your eggs. Feed your babies with grass seed. Go, go. Off there. Off as far as you can." The father tapped the cage gently but the bird held fast to the perch for a moment. Then the pink-tinted downy little creature hobbled out of the cage, its legs crimson in the sunlight. The children closed in to see. It beat its wings but fell to the ground after a few yards. The children clapped their hands and chased it. It flew again, this time more than twenty yards. At the third try it made a bamboo branch and smoothed its feathers with its beak.

The father stayed on at the temple to help put away the pulpit and the other things until late in the afternoon. On the way home he reflected that happiness is funny. If it had weight like coarse sand, he would have collapsed under it halfway home. He wouldn't have the strength to carry it all the way back. But it wasn't like that. Just the opposite. He felt he was floating in the air. The sky above was clear, the land around beautiful. The children tending the water buffalo were playing happily. He hardly noticed the distance to the house. Before he could climb the stairs, he was transfixed by Bunpheng's cry, "Pa, I got lucky today." Proudly, he held up his trophy to show his father. "It was fat and stupid. I beat it down with a stick."

The boy placed his good fortune in his father's hand and turning to the fence shouted, "Hey, there's sister Khaem, Khaem!"

The father dully watched his daughter wearily approaching. The mother came down from the house and began to cry. He gazed stonily at the little bird in his hand, the saffron still showing under its wings.[1]

1969

1. At Vessandara festival time, all the children of the Northeast who have emigrated to the cities long to return home, renew family ties, and give money and other gifts to their parents and relatives. Khaemkham, who had presumably been seduced into the city by the guys in the dark glasses, also felt this urge after three years of silent absence. From her appearance, it is likely her father guessed what had become of her.

SALES REPS FOR THE UNDERWORLD

ยมทูต

THE young man did not quite know what to do. Slowly he walked the length of the narrow path that led in front of the bell tower and the row of monks' living quarters. Everything seemed so quiet and lethargic that it was hard to believe he was inside the compound of a monastery in the city. He saw no sign of life until suddenly a dog appeared from underneath one of the houses. She was trying to escape from her litter of pups, which yelped and ran after her, hitting and missing in their frantic efforts to suckle. Kop stopped to watch as the bitch steadily gained distance from her young and turned the corner, finally going out onto the main street. Left behind, the puppies trotted back under the house.

As the young man looked about undecided, his ears caught the murmur of voices coming from behind the prayer hall. Following the direction of the voices, Kop came upon an elderly monk in conversation with a bricklayer who was repairing the wall of the monastery. With his robe very neatly arranged, the monk had the air of a senior member of the order.

Kop approached him and, to show respect, squatted down before him, placing his palms together.

"Do you have some business here, my son?" the man of religion asked in a kindly voice.

"I would like to visit Phra Thongsa, but I am not sure if he's a monk in this temple."

"Phra Thongsa?" the monk repeated slowly, knitting his brows. "I don't think there is one by that name, my son. What makes you think he is here?"

"I seem to remember the name of the temple and 'Phra Thongsa.'" Again he repeated the name.[1]

"I really don't think there is such a monk at this temple. I doubt if he's here. There are several temples with this name, you know. Does he practice meditation?" The monk looked at the young man as he asked the question.

"I don't know. He left the village many years ago."

"If he meditates then he is probably at the temple on the road to Muang Non. They have an institute there."

"I went there last week. A monk there told me to try here."

"Do you have some urgent business?"

"My brother is sick. He came down to Bangkok to stay with me and get treatment." Kop mentioned the name of a hospital and then fell silent for a few moments. "I would like to ask Phra Thongsa's advice about something. He's a relative of mine."

"Oh, I see. Is the patient very ill then?"

"Well, he's pretty bad."

"Phra Thongsa," the monk said again after a moment's silence. "Which province do you come from?"

"Originally I came from Phanom Phrai District, Roi-Et Province, but now I work in Bangkok."

"In that case, maybe he is Maha Sanit," he said looking towards the row of living quarters. Seeing a couple of novices walking along, he called out, "Say, do you know where Maha Sanit's home village is?"

"Afraid not, Venerable Father."

1. When a person becomes a monk he is given a Pali name, and he may be known either by his personal name or his new name. Hence the confusion.

"Is he from the Northeast? Roi-Et is the Northeast, isn't it?" The latter sentence was said very softly. "We don't know at all, Venerable Father," the novices said, still in response to the original question and walked on.

"And to think they live in the same quarters," the senior monk reflected uncritically.

The bricklayer, who had taken the opportunity to down tools and listen to the conversation, went back to his work.

"But it's probably not the same person. Maha Sanit has been in this temple for a long long time. How long ago did your relative come to Bangkok?"

"About fifteen or sixteen years now. I can't be certain."

"Oh, that long? In that case, why don't you go and ask to make sure?"

The monk walked around the temple building and pointed out the way to Kop. "It's the third house along. You see the room with the window closed? That's it."

Kop gave a reverential gesture of respect to thank the monk and retraced his steps. He stopped at the room, which had been indicated to him, but finding it locked sat down and waited. After a while he felt extremely sleepy as well as thirsty, so he came back down the steps and made his way to a coffee shop.

It was a somber place, built over a pond at one corner of the temple. The owner was a middle-aged man of rather dark complexion, who, when Kop entered, was busy removing liquor bottles from a crate and placing them on wooden shelves against the wall. The man was not wearing a shirt and Kop could easily make out the Monkey God, tigers, and lions above ancient scripts tattooed beneath the beads of sweat on his bare back.

Kop felt reluctant to disturb the owner by ordering something, so he waited until the man turned around and saw him.

"Oh! What would you like?" the man asked, wiping the sweat from his face with the back of his hand.

"Could I have a glass of ice tea, please?" Kop's eyes were on a pot of boiling water, which was gently steaming.

Instead of brewing the tea himself, the man shouted, "Hey, will someone come out and crush the ice?"

The sound of coughing started up from behind the shop. "A bottled drink will do just as well," said the young man changing his mind and giving the brand name of the kind he wanted. The owner of the shop made as though to go for Kop's order, but seeing a woman emerge from inside, returned to his work. The woman who appeared on the scene was about the same age as the man.

"Eh, Lek, now just where did you disappear to?"

The woman did not answer but silently went over to the refrigerator and groped inside for the bottle Kop had asked for. Having found it, she opened it, placed a straw in it, and set it down in front of the young man. She coughed again several times as she made her way back behind the shop. Kop finished the whole bottle at once while gazing down absent-mindedly at the dirty water which flowed sluggishly under the floorboards. The coughing continued intermittently, and Kop noticed then that every time it started the owner of the shop would straighten up and stand very tense until it subsided. As he glanced in Kop's direction, his face was haggard in suffering.

Kop's thoughts turned back to the image of his brother lying on the hospital bed. Time and again Kop had wondered, without coming to any conclusion, who actually suffered most from death—the dead, the dying, or the living?

On several occasions the young man had observed his brother for long periods in an effort to fathom to what extent he suffered, if at all. But there was no way Kop could tell.

When his brother first went into the hospital he used to talk a little about his illness, but he did so without emotion. When he went on to talk about his family, the expression of his voice did not change in any way. In the beginning his brother had Kop write a few letters for him to his wife and family. The contents were nothing extraordinary—just that he was now being taken care of in the hospital and for them not to worry; to take care of the children and the cows and buffaloes and that he would probably soon be well again.

When they were alone, it was his brother who would usually begin a conversation. They would talk about their childhood, about the dry forest and the parched earth where they used to hunt for edible leaves and firewood in the late afternoon. About the time they first noticed the red ball of fire which was the setting sun and were both so scared they ran back crying to the village. Or his brother would remind him of that heavy rainstorm on New Year's night, when they both had to get up in the middle of the night to mend the roof. When they had patched the hole with grass, neither of them could go back to sleep, so they decided to go out into the fields behind their house to hunt frogs. Instead they had come upon an enormous python. When he got to this part in the reminiscence his brother would laugh heartily. "When you saw that snake, your legs just would not move any more. I had to carry you over my shoulder all the way home. Didn't get one single frog."

Even after he had been in the hospital for months and still his condition had not improved, the most his brother would ask Kop to say in letters home would be: "I don't seem to be getting any better, but please don't worry. The doctor is taking good care of me. Even if I do die, please do not be sorry because I'm getting the best medical care." He really did not appear to be upset much.

Kop, on the other hand, fretted, worried, and suffered more than he could put into words and almost beyond endurance.

When his sick brother came down to Bangkok with his card showing he was a World War II veteran, conscripted into service, he was admitted to a government hospital without having to do much string-pulling. A few days later, a skillful doctor had diagnosed the incurable disease and predicted death in a matter of months. Kop remembered very well the ghastly hour when the doctor called him into his office to tell him the result of the tests. There were just the two of them, the doctor and himself. After slowly turning the medical chart back and forth in his hands a few times, the doctor named the disease in an even voice and at the same time told him approximately when the end would come. The young man seemed to hear in that voice, which was both kind and polite, an introduction: "I would like to introduce you to Mr. Death. In about four months' time he will come and take your brother." A chill of emptiness had spread to every pore of his body. The noises of the busy hospital faded; the din of hooting and boat engines on the river sounded as if they were from an alien world. Kop could not remember the state he was in as he left the doctor's office that day.

Although he had complete faith in the doctor's knowledge and ability, there were times when the young man deluded himself by thinking: "No matter how clever a doctor is, he can still make mistakes." It was because of such desperate thoughts that a glimmer of hope and happiness was sometimes born in his heart, but such moments did not last.

Kop had to admit that since he had been separated from his family from the time he was young, under normal circumstances he really did not know what it was like to be lonely. Furthermore, there had been times when he completely forgot that he had a brother. Yet now that Kop knew he and his brother would have to part and that the parting would be forever, he was overwhelmed. For the first time in his life he experienced the feeling of being alone and lonely.

But as the days passed the young man's feelings changed. Perhaps it was because he became accustomed to the ever-present sorrow that the bitterness and emptiness began to give way to pity. There were days when he wished that the living corpse lying on the bed before him would vanish from this world in the wink of an eye. But later a new worry began to gnaw at him and took the place of pity. In his thirty odd years of life, Kop's sole experience of ceremonies connected with death had been as an onlooker at funerals. He had never been in charge. What was he supposed to do now? Worrying about this problem made him forget his grief. He would sit alone silently for hours turning his thoughts back to the village. His sister-in-law lived in a little hut on the edge of the paddy fields. The distance to the main road was half a day's walk. It would be beyond him to take the body back there for the cremation. He had begun thinking about friends in the city, about monks and temples, and it was then that he cheered up a little, for he remembered the name of a monk who was a close relative.

That afternoon Kop lingered in the coffee shop and then walked about in the temple compound until evening. He arrived back at the hospital later than usual as visitors were beginning to leave. He passed a few familiar people at the main gate who smiled and greeted him as usual. When he came to his brother's ward, Kop's heart seemed to shrivel—his brother's bed was missing.

As he stood there confused, a nurse came up and said that his brother had been moved to the room at the end of the corridor. Kop hurried to the small room, which the nurse had indicated, but found his brother asleep. On the bedside table were some fruit, a thermos flask and cans of beverages, some of which had not been there the day before. He himself had not brought all of these things. Many of them were due to the kindness of other patients and their relatives. Some of the patients had been there as long as his brother and had become good friends. When they learned that he came from far away and that his only relative in the city was Kop, these people were touching in their generosity, some even returning to visit him after their discharge.

But, Kop reflected, there were two people who were especially kind to his brother, the two elderly gentlemen whom he had just passed at the main gate. Kop remembered seeing those two from the early days when he brought his brother in. At first he thought they must be members of the hospital staff but then he noticed that some days they brought with them bags of fruit and drinks, so he came to the conclusion that they too must be visiting a patient. Whenever these two walked past his brother's bed they would stop to ask how he felt and chat about other things for a few moments. Some days they even brought fruit for him.

That evening, as his brother slept through the visiting hour, Kop did not have a chance to chat. He walked back alone silently. When compared with the daytime, the atmosphere of the hospital was rather melancholy. The inner doors were already closed and the only people left were visitors who lingered until the last possible minute.

Before reaching the main gate, Kop walked by a couple of nurses who were just coming on duty and the doctor who had told him about his brother's illness four months before. The doctor did not seem to remember him. He almost did not recognize the doctor either, as he had not seen him again since that day. Indeed, he had thought that maybe the doctor was no longer at the hospital as he had read and heard that the really good doctors often went to work in America.

In the bus on his way home, the young man recalled how dejected the doctor looked as he disappeared into the darkness of the hospital building. During these months of daily visits to the hospital, Kop's experience told him that the doctors were very special men. Their faces were at all times completely impassive, no matter whether they were dealing with sickness or death. Kop had wondered what their hearts could be made of.

His thoughts went back to the time when he was a boy and used to herd the buffaloes. When one wandered off and he knew it could be found, he would spend the rest of the day looking for it; but if he felt that it had been stolen, he'd abandon the search. But a doctor, even knowing that a patient had no hope of living, continued to care for him with that expressionless face, as if such care were nothing unusual.

The next day was a holiday and when Kop arrived at the hospital there were more visitors crowding around than usual. When he entered the sick room he saw a man standing by the bed. He was neatly dressed—a white long-sleeved shirt, a navy blue tie, and dark trousers. He was looking with great interest at Kop's brother. As Kop approached the bed, the man turned and smiled.

"You're early today. Of course, it's Sunday."

"Yes," Kop answered, trying to think where he had seen the man before.

"Are you related to the patient?" His tone intimated that he was a hospital official. Kop suddenly remembered that he had seen the man walking about the hospital.

"I'm his brother. There are just the two of us."

Kop's brother opened his eyes and tried to look around. His condition had obviously deteriorated since the day before. His lips moved to form Kop's name silently, while tears filled his sunken eyes. The sadness which had left Kop for a while yesterday gushed back into his heart. He took his brother's hand in his. There was a lump in his throat as he tried to stifle a sob.

"Don't take it so hard," a soft voice came to him from behind. Then silence hung over the scene for a long time.

"Have you made any preparations?" The stranger spoke again. This time the tone of his voice was different.

"Are you going to wait or cremate immediately?"

"What did you say?" Kop looked up.

"Do you plan to keep it a while or cremate it immediately?"

"Plan to keep what?"

"The body. Your brother's body. Have you made any arrangements for the cremation at any temple yet?"

"Listen, you! My brother's not dead yet." The young man's lips were trembling and his ears rang so loudly that he did not hear his own voice, but before the flames of anger and resentment could burst from him, two men entered the room.

They were the two he had passed at the gate the day before and who had always been so kind to his brother.

"How are things?" They greeted him with natural cheerfulness, but when they saw the expression on Kop's face, they both turned to look with reproach at the other man.

"Try not to take it so hard," one of the two said, shifting his gaze from Kop to the patient who was barely breathing. The other man backed away and then went out.

"You haven't made an agreement with him already, have you?"

"Agreement about what?" Kop asked.

"Sorry, I thought you had already discussed it with him." His voice had become gentler.

"What are you talking about?"

"Listen, don't be too ready to settle anything with him. He's a decoy, a con man—gets a cut from the temple."

Kop's cheekbones stuck out as he clenched his teeth and he had difficulty in breathing.

"When the time comes you'd do better to call on our services. Our temple is just near here. We also provide you with a hearse and a coffin to boot."

The breeze off the river brought damp fresh air through the open window.

"Our charges are lower than other places, too."

The voice droned on in tones, now high, now low, that seemed to come from far away.

"You can choose from our price range—eight hundred to two thousand baht, plain caskets quite cheap—gilded rather more expensive—different sizes of wreaths and floral offerings also available, to suit all purses—entertainment also provided at very reasonable rates—only the most scholarly monks employed for chanting . . ."

The hours flowed by. Kop sat on a bench on the riverbank gazing drearily at the traffic on the busy river. The gloom that had shrouded his heart was beginning to lift. He began thinking of the money in his wallet and again felt irritable. Actually, it was quite near the end of the month. If his brother could only hold on for half a week more, Kop knew he could manage to wheel his brother's body through the temple gate at the lowest rate quoted.

Suddenly the doctor entered his thoughts again. Then he felt hungry so he walked outside to the market for a dish of rice and curry. He loitered in the market all afternoon. He was afraid to go back into the hospital, but at the same time he could not just go away like a coward.

It was almost dark by the time he made up his mind to return. His heart was beating very fast as he mounted the stairs. When he came in sight of his brother's room, he became numb and could not move. At the same time, he saw a pair of sharp eyes staring at him and heard a voice from inside the room saying: "There he is; he's just come back."

There was a sudden commotion in that narrow little room. Several faces turned and looked through the door at once, as though at a given signal.

Kop made a quick about-turn, scrambled down the stairs and headed straight for the main gate leading to the street.

In a moment calm returned to the sick room. One of the men wearing the yellow robe of a Buddhist monk, bewildered, asked in a Northeastern accent: "Are you sure he's my relative?"

"I wouldn't know, but this is the man named Kap from Roi-Et and his younger brother is called Kop."[2]

1970

2. Not long before Khamsing wrote this story, his younger brother, Sian, still in his twenties and recently married, died of cancer of the liver in Siriraj Hospital located on the bank of the Chao Phraya River.

HAPPY BIRTHDAY, GRANDPA

แฮ็ปปี้เบิร์ธเดย์ คุณตา

BEFORE, whenever I went to a Thai movie, I would get the feeling I was in a fantasy world. On the screen, for the first few minutes, the geography, the events, and the faces—everything, in fact—looked pretty familiar, but after a little while when actors I knew began to act bizarre, you know, surreal, the feeling of familiarity would give way to bewilderment. And I would marvel at how the producer and director managed to put together such a far-out story with such weird people.

But now I must apologize to all of those involved in the Thai film industry. I am writing this story with a sense of guilt and with real respect for their genius. It was wrong of me to think the absurdity was something special only to Thai films (circa 1971) because, actually that is not so. Laugh at those who say to you that Thai movies are somehow inane and dated. Thai moviemakers may be short on funds and box-office stars, but in finding cutting-edge stories and scripts, they are out in front.

However, you can be sure that if they are not on their toes. Thai society is going to zip past them left and right and if they do not pick up the new eccentricities, they will soon be outdated.

The rainy season this year, especially in the lower Northeast, was terrifically dry and hot. The rains had failed from July to the end of August. So when an old friend stopped by to ask me to keep him company on a visit to his old hometown, I was a little reluctant. On the one hand I wanted to go because I hadn't been there in a long time, but the thought of having to trudge under the hot sun for a whole day put me off. However, when he said he was homesick, I felt for him and couldn't refuse.

When we got there I realized my forecast about the discomfort of the trip was way off. Instead of having to walk for thirty kilometers like ten years before, we had only a stretch of less than ten. The Rural Accelerated Development people had scraped away the grass and thrown up some sandy soil to make a track in the direction of the village. The convenience was a problem, though, because we figured on spending a whole day in getting there and now we had to think of some way of killing the afternoon. In the rainy season, you can hardly find a soul in a village during the day, so we dawdled at a coffee shop in town until the afternoon and then continued on. As soon as we got off the local bus and started on our walk, my friend began telling me about the places and folks we passed. He greeted everyone, some rightly, some wrongly. Some returned the greeting with a blank look until it dawned on them who he was.

I made polite noises but wasn't particularly excited as my own life had been spent going back and forth from city to country. However I did watch for the changes from when I was a kid. Except for a general decline, things did not appear to me to be much different. I saw ribs. A man's ribs can tell you something about how he is faring. Let me tell you I had the chance to see the ribs of these people in high relief. The teachers in the village might set themselves apart with their fine uniforms but most of the folks stuck to the old ways wearing only an old pair of loose pants knotted at the waist or sarong with a *phakhaoma* slung over one shoulder exposing the chest. What I saw of progress were the nylon dipnets and plastic baskets that groups of villagers were swishing back and forth in the ponds to trap tadpoles and baby fish.

Although my friend had been excited all along, when he had

taken in this scene he became depressed. Without the sour moonshine to help, supper would have been decidedly blah. By the time the meal was over, he had perked up and got talkative, rambling from one thing to another, getting a high from hearing himself talk. And then, just like that, without any fanfare, he stopped and like someone possessed by music began reciting the names of world-famous composers and making remarks that were totally out of place. Our drinking companions looked at one another like, what's going on? Actually, I had heard the strains of music since early evening and thought it odd but couldn't figure out what it was until my friend got turned on. It was the music that set him off. I hadn't expected to hear serious classical music in this backwater of our Thailand. I cocked my ear for a moment and the music started up again. My friend exclaimed as if probing, "Tschaikovsky? Tschaikovsy."

I asked some questions and learned a celebration was going on in the village. Not a housewarming or a wedding as I thought it would be. No, it was simply a birthday party for a school headmaster. He wasn't giving himself a party to show off; no sir, in the honeyed language of the M.C. who was one of his daughters, it was a "demonstration of filial gratitude presented to our dear father."

By listening carefully, I got the details. Not only were his children offering their felicitations many times over, but also the grandchildren were going to put on a little show to congratulate their grandfather. The M.C.'s announcement made me want to take a look so I took leave and by following the sound of the music reached the party house—a small wooden affair rather brightly lit with lanterns. A good look at what was going on showed it was just a lovely little domestic gathering—family members getting together to give a party for their dad. But there it is—we Thai are so generous that whatever we do we cannot help but think of others. Thus, when the family merely wanted

to give a party for their father, they had the heart to point the
loudspeaker in the direction of the village to spread the festivity
around. The villagers responded enthusiastically, children and
grown-ups bringing their mats and laying them out all over the
front yard of the house and spilling out onto the road. Not a few
perched on the rails of the buffalo pen. I myself settled on the
beam of a foot-operated rice-pounder on the other side of the
road.

It was one of the cutest spectacles I'd seen. I got caught up in
the succession of moving images like I was in a dream. They
were mostly dances representing different animals in the style of
a ballet in harmony with the classical music. Each variation was
accompanied by a commentary: "And next on the program is
Dancing Butterflies." She said the title in English. "In Thai it
means *phi sua*," she added.

"In our dialect, we say *maengkabia,*" the male M.C. cut in.

"Right," she continued. "The performers for the next item are
our very own favorite stars from the first number, there's O, Nui,
Puk and Taem. Our little Tum will play the rose."

A sweet chubby girl of about three wearing a red dress stepped
slowly to the middle of the open veranda and plunked herself
down. She was followed by a gaggle of little girls of about the
same age, each dressed in a white blouse with a bouffant pleated
skirt dotted with spots. They circled around the little rose girl
flapping their arms up and down in time with the music that
blared from the tape recorder.

More remarkable, in addition to the commentary on the
different numbers, between the acts the M.C. expatiated on the
fine qualities of her father both by way of praise and felicitation.
"Father is a hero to his children. He is a paragon of diligence and
patience. He chose the path of hardship and poverty so that his
children might succeed in life. Though only a primary school
teacher, he is not a simple person to be looked down on. His

children went to school and three received degrees from the hand of the king, one to become a university lecturer, one a . . ."

The M.C.'s lengthy encomiums awakened in me a respect for the man and I thought I'd like to see what he looked like and make his acquaintance. I tried but couldn't pick him out of the crowd. I stayed to see a few more acts and was beginning to despair of seeing him when, getting ready to leave, I heard the syrupy M.C. say that it was getting pretty late and the stars of the show were getting sleepy and some had already fallen asleep so for the last number all the grandchildren would sing a final congratulations to their grandfather. She invited the teacher to come and sit in the middle of the veranda. I was in luck. A man past his prime, hair close-cropped, wearing only a silk sarong and a *phakhaoma* tied around his waist, got up from the first row of spectators and walked straight into the center of the veranda. A group of about eight grandchildren rushed around him and up swelled the congratulatory song. In English they sang, "Happy birthday, happy birthday, happy birthday to Grandpa."

1971

PARADISE PRESERVED

สวรรค์ยังอยู่

AND so it is. Paradise is still preserved in Thailand. At least that's the position of the prominent experts who participated in a panel discussion on Thailand's economic problems at Chulalongkorn University auditorium at the beginning of this month.

The reason why there are many things in society that seem a bit uncertain and shoddy, the respected panelists explained, is because our Thai gods have not been very good. While I sat there and listened, I hesitated to agree with them wholeheartedly. Thinking of the pale faces of friends from various walks of life that I observed almost daily, the paradise to my mind had already been lost. But though I am not a ready believer, those experts seemed to be more impressive than house lizards or geckoes.[1]

And after having observed the ways and means of my own friends and other people, I began to agree with the experts' opinions—especially the part that referred to the gods. At least I had to admit to myself that I had witnessed various happenings that supported such ideas.

One case was that of a former neighbor whose fate almost turned him into a brothel owner. But, by the skin of his teeth, some god had managed to save him.

In fact, it seems that another deity has been added to Thailand's stock of them.

---

1. This refers to a traditional Thai belief about the cries of a house lizard or gecko being omens of misfortune if uttered when one is leaving one's house.

The story goes like this. The neighbor friend was originally a schoolteacher. He worked diligently at his profession for twenty consecutive years. His fortune was what might be expected for an ordinary government official of his age. He had a house of his own. As he had more children, his house came to be too small and crowded, and his family expenses increased every day until he had difficulty making ends meet. Finally, thinking about the problems he faced, he considered looking for a new livelihood. He decided to resign from government service in order to collect his retirement bonus. He calculated that it was sufficient to build a rather large house for his family. He then applied for a job on an American military base.

Compared to the old job, his new income was rather high, and he expected that his household would turn into a paradise overnight. At the same time, the town he lived in was booming. It was exploding with life and color. But along with this, the cost of living also boomed, and the paradise that he thought would be coming over the horizon seemed to be receding into the distance. However, because of the familiarity and sensitive understanding that he had developed toward his new friends (in fact, masters or gods) he was in a better position than most. So he divided his big house and rented a room to one of his new friends.

After a while, the manner in which this friend spent his leisure time at home made my old neighbor rather uneasy, since his children were just entering puberty. He could evict his new friend, but then, he could also use the rent. In the end, he took his wife and children back to their old small house, leaving the big house as a gathering place for the descendants of the god Mars and the angels from the nearby hamlets.[2] So my teacher friend, a lowly man, had the privilege of owning a carnal paradise.

2. In the original Thai text, "Jupiter," written as a transliteration of the Western name, is used instead of "Mars."

114

All was well until the time of the withdrawal of the gallant American troops. My friend's paradise plunged downward in this new era. We met occasionally. When I mentioned the changing situation, his look was serious. But there was a trace of a smile on his face as he stated in tones designed to persuade me (and himself) that the situation was not yet critical. Much of the military crowd had already left but plenty of replacements had also arrived. Would an ally let an ally down? His voice was sure and firm. His big house still had tenants, one after another. The girls were there all the time to attend to his business interests. It was not until our ally began to close down its bases that the happiness and contentment on his face disappeared completely. In this situation of panic and disorder, it is hard to say in which part of the Dharma[3] my friend took refuge to control himself so that, without hysterics, he could endure the weight of his own paradise crumbling down in front of him.

Many months later, we met again. This time he was driving a black-license-plate taxi transporting passengers up the hill.[4] He dropped by to visit and talk about his decline.

"The young ones had to leave school. The oldest one finished vocational school, but she can't find a job yet, and she's behaving as if she hates home," he said, talking of his children.

I asked about the house he rented out. He shook his head. "It was closed down," he said. "In fact, I didn't do it. The authorities did. I could have kept it open if I was willing to pay them off regularly, but I didn't think that was worthwhile pursuing. So for now I'm trying this." He meant his taxi. "But there's hardly anything left after you have paid for daily and monthly queue fees, fees to those who operate the depots, toll charges, and also

3. Buddhist canon or belief.
4. A "black-license-plate taxi" is an illegal taxi; legal taxis carry yellow license plates.

service charges for the 'gods.'[5] I am now applying to get back into the civil service."

It is true what the experts say. There are gods in Thai society. The last time I saw this friend of mine, he had changed so much—but only for the better. His thin face was now filled out and beaming with the signs of well being. When he talked, his voice was vigorous with a ring of authority. He was a new man.

The change was very much a surprise, but if you looked deeper at the cause, it was not so surprising, because in this society of ours power comes from mysterious sources.

My friend related to me that his running around for readmission into government service had brought him into close contact with an important person who could be counted as a kind of god—a member of parliament (from the "Can-Do-It" Party).[6] Those who have ever believed in the moon and the stars would claim that it was my friend's lucky star that was guiding him, since at the time he went to see the MP, the MP was planning his campaign for the upcoming election.

As it happened, my friend was rather gifted at the art of rhetoric. At least that was the result of his having to use it in his work with school children for twenty years. This gift probably gave the honorable representative the idea that my friend could be useful in his next campaign. His application for readmission into government service was accepted with no difficulty whatsoever.

Every time I think of the story of my friend's life, the words of an author I once read come to mind. He said simply: "Life is a journey." I am not sure whether my teacher friend has read these

5. In this instance, any official who can pull his weight.
6. The fact that this is the slogan of the Social Action Party, in power during 1975–1976 is fortuitous. The "Can-Do-It" Party did not come into existence until well after this story was first published.

words, but the way he has been carrying on seems to indicate that he knows them by heart. Since the day he found his new path—which took him, carrying a file, from the MP's house to his new office in this government department—he has made scores of journeys of the same sort. (Of course, the journey of a lackey is an ageless journey.) The distance he has traveled back and forth from his office to the MP's, carrying letters of authority to departmental offices, schools, and universities (seeking admission for certain students) would probably measure half the length of the continent. The more he travels the more firm is his place in the inner circle and the more clout he wields.

Being the MP's man, he is now respected and feared in and beyond the district. If somehow a spell turned his small world into one of animals, this friend of mine would have the status of a crow in a herd of cattle with sores on their backs.[7] But since his world is populated with humans, he has the status of a superman. For the time being, I would call him a man who casts a shadow that is not his own.

1973

7. In fighting, bulls sometimes get wounds on their backs in places where they cannot be licked clean. If maggots appear, crows will fly down to peck at the wound causing considerable pain. Thus, at the mere appearance of a crow, a herd that includes bulls with sores on their backs may take off in fright. The crow has thus acquired an occult power. Applied to people, the Thai expression meaning literally "a bull (or cow) with an open wound on its back" may be translated "a skeleton in the closet" or something that is better kept hidden.

I LOST MY TEETH

ฟันผมหาย

WHEN he first greeted me in a sullen voice with the question: "Why don't you ask what happened to my teeth?" I was struck dumb for a time not knowing what to say. In fact I had noticed the deformity on his pale face when I first glanced at him. Even so, my brain was not fast enough to come up with an answer to the sudden question. I did not know how to incorporate a greeting into a reply so as to keep the atmosphere easy and to avoid hurting his feelings any further.

Actually, I had heard a bit about his misfortune, but the information was superficial and confusing. It had been passed on by word of mouth and you could not be sure how accurate it was. The first wave of rumor indicated he had been shot dead; then it changed to his having been shot almost dead but having survived. It was not until I met him personally and heard the story from his own mouth that I knew that all he actually received was a blow to the face. The whole thing might be called a trivial matter compared to other robberies—considering he lost only two hundred and some baht, an old pistol, and four teeth. A sporting person would say that people give away more than that to their friends. But then it is only a small matter to me because it was not I who lost two hundred baht, an old pistol, and four teeth. For the person who did, the tired and gloomy face and the odd sounds pouring through his deformed oral cavity seemed to express a different viewpoint. After listening to him grumble away for a while, I offered my own unsympathetic opinion. "You had the gun with you. Why did you let them strike you so easily?"

I had not yet finished speaking when his face, which a moment before had recovered its calm, turned back to scowling. His sunken eyes flashed a piercing glance.

"I bought the thing with just that thought in mind: to protect myself against robbers and thieves. But you know, nowadays things around here are so confusing. You can't tell who's a bad guy and who's a good one. Come out and live here for a while—you'll see what I mean. Especially a village like ours that's in the jungle. People outside seem so worried about us. Week after week and month after month we have to mold a smile on our faces with no time to look normal. Like idiots, we smile back at everybody who turns up to visit us. They come right into our kitchens to find out how we are doing, to make our acquaintance, to ask about our livelihood. Question after question. Some come from the subdistrict office; some come from the offices of the district, province, or the capital, and some come from the outside world, from places nobody has ever even heard of. Every one of them seems to have the same forced smile like they all learned it from the same teacher. When the good guys can smile, the bad guys can, too. Then what use can a gun be . . . ?

"That afternoon, the day I lost my teeth, these people filed through the gate, all with broad grins on their faces. One of them came straight to where I was shoveling husks from under the storehouse. Another went toward the pigsty where my wife and my little son were pouring bran into the trough. Three gathered in front of the stairs to the house. I looked up and smiled. Before the smile had spread fully over my lips, a gun was nudged into my waist and I was ordered to put the hoe down . . .

"At that instant, the three who were waiting at the foot of the stairs all ran up into the house and started searching for things they might fancy. I was stupefied by this for a while. When I recovered, I got enraged. My eyes became blurred with the tears that were welling up as I watched the three of them moving around upstairs. So I said, 'If you are so brave and bold, why are you picking on people like me who live from hand to mouth? Why don't you go and rob those people who are rolling in wealth?'"

"'Who?'"

"'Those moneymen and millionaires who ride around in big cars and walk with their bellies sticking out in . . .' Before I could finish my sentence, the bastard swung the gunstock at my mouth and snapped, 'What a loud mouth.' I was laid out at his feet with four of my teeth stuck down my throat."

"Did you report this to the authorities?"

"Yes."

"What did they say?"

"Nothing. They just acknowledged my report."

"Did you tell them the details?"

"Yes, every detail. Oh, but I didn't tell them what I said before they hit me."

"Why not?"

"Like I said, everything is mixed up these days and you can't tell who's a good guy and who's a bad guy. Who knows what would have happened? I might have lost all the rest of my teeth."

1973

THE BUFFALO WITH THE RED HORNS

ควายเขาแดง

"THANONCHAI" was not really the family name of Mr. Si or, as the local folks called him, "Thit Si."[1] But because he was a fellow so smart and full of ideas to the point of eccentricity, many of the things he did became the subject of jokes for the people thereabouts. And this led his acquaintances to append "Thanonchai"[2] to his name. It caught on and eventually everyone called him "Si Thanonchai" or "Thit Si Thanonchai" as they pleased.

Although calling him that did carry an edge of ridicule, it did not bother our subject. Indeed, it seemed sometimes as if he had forgotten it was a kind of nickname for when someone would call him by his real first and family names, he would seem bewildered for a moment before responding. But if someone called him "Mr. Si Thanonchai" he would reply without any hesitation, certain it was he who was being addressed.

He was a country fellow whose livelihood was just like that of the rest—rice farming. And, as for nearly all of them, being happy or unhappy, well off or poorly off, depended on rain.

1. In Thailand, it is customary to call people by their first name. If one is being formal, as one nearly always is, the title "Mr." or *Thit* is used with the first name rather than the family name. *Thit* is a title of respect for someone who has been a monk.

2. Si Thanonchai is the name of a popular, legendary savant who benefits himself and sometimes his princely employer by his foxy ingenuity.

Rain, therefore, was the true god who could make life good or bad.

Even though his intelligence and wit enabled him to find ways to get by rather better than his fellow rice farmers of that county, when the god neglected him for a number of years running, his family was hit hard and on the verge of going under.

The misfortune to come was, in one respect, due to his being a sticker unlike most of the other farmers of that county; he held on to his buffalo. Most of his friends, although continuing to farm, sold their buffaloes in exchange for rice to eat. When planting season came, they would rent a buffalo that sometimes was their own animal, to pull the plow and harrow. In time it became the custom. This buying and selling, renting and hiring, established a familiar dependency between the Chinese entrepreneur and the farmers. As time went on, farming took on the character of planting paddy to exchange for polished rice. Practically all of Thit Si's neighbors sold their buffalo to the Chinese merchant who was the owner of the big rice mill in the nearby town.

As time passed, the relationship became deeper and their merchant transferred his house registration to the village itself. When the post of village headman became vacant, he put himself forward as the candidate. And later on, when the post of county headman was made empty, he put himself up for election to that too. The combined power of money and rice was enough to insure that no one dared to challenge him. He could thus be said to have been elected county headman unanimously, not something one comes across very often.

In the beginning, in order to sell their buffaloes, Thit Si's neighbors would have to lead them to the merchant's stock pen in the market town. When it came time for plowing, they would go and enter a rental agreement and take the buffaloes back. If the rains came normally, they would keep the buffaloes until the end of the planting season. But if the rains failed, they would return the buffaloes, arrange to postpone payment of the rent and interest, and go off to find jobs wherever they could.

This mutual trade and hiring out prospered to such an extent that soon the Chinese merchant found that he had more buffaloes than he could keep. His financial position improved until he became one of the magnates of the district and his social position, given his affluence and offices, fit the newly popular saying: "With money, the rest comes easy." In particular, the office of county headman gave the merchant power and influence and made a lot of things easy.

That was why, with the buffaloes crowding the holding pen, the farmers were no longer required to lead their buffaloes all the way into town and take them back again. If a farmer intended to keep the buffalo for the next growing season, the powerful Chinese merchant—county headman would simply send a few of his henchmen, of whom he had many by now, out to the village to paint the base of the buffalo's horns red as a sign that it was now his property.

To go back to the story of Thit Si, after several years of trying this, that, and the other thing contrary to local usage, he began to think that continuing to keep his buffalo just for plowing was a burden. No matter how hard-pressed he was, it kept him from going off to find work elsewhere like his neighbors did. But while he thought about selling, he felt sorry for his children who loved the animal and he could not bring himself to part with it. He worried about this for several days until one day he laughed to himself like someone who has seen the light and headed off to the market town returning just before dark.

The next morning, Thit Si's son rode his buffalo with bright red bands around the base of the horns off to join all the other red-marked buffaloes heading for the pastureland.

A few days later, Si set out to find a job in another town leaving his wife and children to take care of the buffalo and watch the house until his return. He had no worry about thieves and cattle rustlers, for he was certain that no miscreant would dare to touch a buffalo with the red marking.

Our Thit Si had not been away for long before two downpours thoroughly flooded the area. So he hurried home and set to work in the fields with his wife and children. Not yet halfway into the rainy season they completed the transplanting of the rice seedlings into the paddy fields. From then on Si enjoyed a happy idleness waiting for the plants to mature. Two months later, at the end of the rainy season when the earth began to dry out, Si's fields were replete with rich golden ears of rice bending over ready for the sickle's cutting edge. When the ground was dry enough, Thit Si cleared and prepared a small plot for use as a threshing floor and the whole family pitched in to do the harvest. Before long the sheaves of rice were stacked in a mound on the threshing floor looking like a huge anthill.

Just when the family were relishing their success, one morning, out of the blue, a familiar visitor walked over to the edge of the threshing ground and after the usual pleasantries began conversing in a serious vein.

"Look here, Thit Si, if I remember correctly you have about nine acres of paddy field. Would that be right?"

"That's correct, Deputy."

The visitor cast his eye over the sheaves of rice that covered the whole of the threshing floor. "Well, now, that being the case, the rent for the buffalo comes to exactly fifty-six bushels of paddy."

Si winced like a temple boy who had just been caned on his backside. "What! I . . . I don't . . ." Words failed him as he realized that the neighbor, standing in front of him, was not only the assistant headman of the village, but was also an important henchman of the Chinese merchant–county headman. In that village he was also the big guy's overseer, his deputy, his eyes and ears, and his collector of rent for the buffaloes and paddy fields.

"What do you mean 'you don't'?"

"It's got nothing to do with me," replied Si tentatively.

"Look at your buffalo, for Pete's sake!"

"My buffalo is not involved."

"Not involved you say. Just take a look at the horns."

This assault based on the evidence rattled the owner of the threshing floor. The wit that used to come so easily practically vanished. When Si recovered all he could say was "Honestly, it doesn't concern you."

"Come on, the horns speak for themselves." When Si remained silent, the big merchant's man got more aggressive and in a mocking tone continued, "So I suppose you're saying your buffalo's horns made themselves red."

"No, they didn't become like that by themselves. I painted them that way myself."

"What did you say?"

"I painted them with my own hands. I've still got the can of leftover paint in the granary."

After looking him in the face for a spell, the overseer gave a little laugh. "You're nuts. Only a fool would think of doing something weird like that."

"I'm no fool. I just painted the horns to keep away the thieves. You know how it is, Deputy."

As the talk took an uncomfortably close turn, the mocking expression disappeared, and the henchman continued darkly, "I know everyone else in the village calls you 'Si Thanonchai' but I've never called you that."

"You can call me that if you like, Deputy, I don't mind," Si replied. "But what I said is the truth. I'll swear to it at any temple you like. That buffalo is still mine. I haven't sold it. Not yet."

Appreciating that Si was prepared to take an oath on it, the assistant headman backed off. "Think it over, Thit Si. It would do you no good to cheat somebody like the county chief. Who knows, one day you may be without enough to eat."

"It's because I am thinking about being hard up that I'm talking to you like this, Deputy." Si paused for a moment. "But I don't want to argue with you. I know that in these things the big man is serious and a decent guy. Go back and ask him whether or not I sold my buffalo to him."

Later that day, the deputy quietly went off and the affair seemed closed. Thit Si thought that it would go no further. But a few days after that, when the Chinese merchant cum county headman's overseer summoned him to a meeting at the village headman's house, Thit Si knew the case was not yet over. The deputy's name was "Mr. Mouse" and he had a pointed face like a pygmy shrew. As a monk, he advanced in his studies until he almost became the temple abbot. And he had the verbal facility of a preacher. Si's heart was beating fast as he followed Overseer Mouse to the village headman's house and by the time he got there he was still tense. There on the open verandah Thit Si saw the Chinese merchant–county headman sitting importantly at his ease with one leg crossed over the other. Like the other county headmen who spread money around to buy the villagers' votes, he did not talk much. When Thit Si raised his hands together in respectful greeting, instead of returning the greeting in the same fashion, the big man merely acknowledged it with a nod and let his Overseer Mouse open the floodgates.

"This business of the rent for the buffalo is over with," the sharp-faced man began. "But this smart-ass, tomfoolery painting

126

your own buffalo's horns with red, that was wrong. You had the nerve to pass that animal off without any right. That is a serious matter and an affront, which County Headman here can allow no one to get away with. By now everyone knows that every buffalo with horns marked in red belongs to the county headman. If we let just anybody do like you did, people would become confused to the point where the red horn would lose its sanctity. Anybody might think that red-marked buffaloes belong to ordinary villagers and not to the county headman and then they might become game for thieves and rustlers.

"Be that as it may, this stupid effrontery of yours appears to be only the first time and so the county headman is going to forgive you. But he has called you here in the presence of the village headman and the other folks to give a bond of good behavior. If you are ever such a fool as to do a thing like that again, not only will you have to pay the rent, but your buffalo will be seized as well."

Overseer Mouse took a deep breath before continuing. "Nevertheless—and this is a kindness—you, Thit Si, will have to cover the cost of your own folly by paying the county headman's gasoline bill for coming here amounting to one hundred baht."

Seeing the affair that started off all right end up like this and getting angry over being repeatedly labeled a fool, Thit Si raised his voice and argued back. "Look, I may not have done the right thing, but I am not a fool. We are all from this place. The overseer's insulting me like that is out of place."

"Oh, so Thit Si thinks he was being clever?" the assistant headman retorted.

"Sure."

The overseer stroked the edge of his knife-sharp nose like he was thinking before continuing in a severe tone. "Alright then, you can pay for your cleverness with a nice big bottle of whisky to go with the headman's chicken soup. How about that, Village Headman?"

"Good, good" clamored the village folks who came to act as witnesses. At the same time, the Chinese merchant–county headman nodded repeatedly to show approval of the judgment of his overseer.

1981

INTERCOURSE

ประเวณี

ALL these village folks counted themselves related in some way and had always shared the good and the bad. So why did the incident become baneful, deeply embarrassing, and cause estrangement to the point where eventually they could not look one another in the eye? The reason was surely that they had known Somdet since he was a baby, recognized him as one of their own, and knew what sort of person he was.

Mind you, Somdet wasn't such a fool that he didn't make sense when you talked to him. True, he was dropped from primary school because he got too old for compulsory schooling. But later, when the government decided to put an end to illiteracy, Somdet passed the test just like the others, because he could point correctly to consonants and vowels and to some words made up from them, as well as to the numbers one to ten written on the blackboard. It was all in accordance with the rules and so he got his official certificate of literacy from the government.

But how he passed was the source of jokes like how the committeeman hand-signaled so hard that he got a cramp in his arm (somebody claimed they saw him take out a jar of Tiger Balm and massage his shoulder with it). They said the reason why the official went to so much trouble was, in the first place, to gain favor with the village headman sitting next to him. The headman was rooting for Somdet and sweating with the effort to get awarded the big sign saying "Illiteracy-Free Village" which the committee had already prepared to set up along the road leading into the hamlet. In the second place, the members of the committee themselves wanted to get the credit which would lead to salary hikes and promotions, following long-established custom.

The village headman could not contain his joy at Somdet's success. At first, Somdet himself was pretty nervous. But a little way into the exam, he began to get a kick out of it. The sympathetic onlookers cheered and clapped when he would point to the right letter and he would guffaw. The headman, who had been looking grumpy for weeks ever since he learned the date of the examination, was wreathed in smiles. Since this had the nature of a competition among villages, a question of gaining or losing face was involved. And where face is in question, everyone is sure to probe the others' weak points. They would send spies off to seek out the other villages' dumbbells and counted them as minus points. In this respect, Somdet was the cause of the headman's moodiness and miserable expression. So the moment the committeeman called out "Mr. Somdet passes," the headman forgot himself and jumped up grinning hugely; the pallor of the past few days was replaced with fine color like he just had a draft of fresh blood from out of a pig's neck. The unequivocal declaration of the committee was a pick-me-up. And from then on, everyone in the village began to call Somdet "Mister Somdet."

While the effort of the government that day officially removed the stigma of illiteracy, it did not do much to erase the old Somdet, for every time someone in the village saw something weird going on or saw someone get muddled or put things the wrong way, he'd say, "Oh they're doing a Somdet," and then laugh.

If you look at the thing dispassionately you would say that particularly the older villagers felt ashamed later on because they had been convinced that Somdet was peculiar and assumed he was not quite right in the head. They disparaged him, made fun of him, and made him the butt of their little jokes. So afterwards, when they saw with their own eyes Somdet give medical treatment that saved the life of one of their aged relatives—a man so ill the doctor had shaken his head in despair—they were nonplussed, they could not laugh any more. Despite the fact that a few people persisted in saying that what he had done was still "a Somdet," the result of his doctoring skill silenced those who had been so fond of puffing to gain face, inflating amounts of five to ten, of ten to a hundred, and then upping to a thousand. Thus, when the incident occurred which changed their positions, nearly everyone felt they had been caught with their pants down in the middle of a temple fair.

It began to unfold late one afternoon halfway into the rainy season. Earlier in the day, a bedraggled Somdet returned to the village in a friend's motorized cart coming from the market town. His journey home didn't start in the town but rather in a logging camp deep in the jungle on the mountains the other side of the frontier. It was a precipitous trip, sudden and agitated.

The trip itself began when Somdet got up drowsily one morning, and got ready to boil some water for his boss. Normally two of his buddies, local boys,[1] would get up before dawn to make some food for the workers. As the boss was a late riser, Somdet would wait until they were finished before putting the kettle on. So he was surprised to see, instead of a fire in the cooking hearth, a heap of cold gray ash. He got washed and did his other business, including giving the flies behind the bushes their morning meal, but still saw no trace of the two locals. He

1. The logging is going on in the shadowy border area between Thailand and Cambodia in the aftermath of the Khmer Rouge defeat. The "locals" are Cambodian-speaking.

sidled up to the small hut, a little way away, and saw the door shut. Only the sound of a radio filtered faintly through the door. Somdet left and sat down for a while but when the two did not come out, he went back for a look inside. He pushed open the plaited bamboo door and saw nothing but the little radio lying on its side on the floor sending out hoarse news reports. For a moment, he stared at the radio, puzzled, and then left. While lighting the fire he suddenly thought of his two pals and the little radio again.

For the first few days, neither Somdet nor those two Khmer camp-mates had been able to communicate much. So the boss got a radio for them all to listen to; but since they spoke different languages and he was alone, the radio was always tuned into the language of the other two who finally took it over. When eventually both sides learned enough to talk to each other, the two locals recounted the almost daily radio reports of fighting in the jungle, far off and nearby.

Somdet finally realized that his two buddies from the jungle had quietly slipped away. Although he was not one to think far into the future, the fact that he had twice been in camps that had been set on fire led him to imagine that something pretty bad might be going to happen.

The job they had hired him for, given his build, brains, and straight-as-an-arrow ingenuousness, was regular camp watch-man. But after several months, when the boss's personal servant got sick and took home leave, Somdet, who often hung around the kitchen, was asked to take a kettle of hot water to his boss. "So you know how to boil water, do you?" the boss asked him. Somdet only laughed out loud without answering the question, but to everyone else he commented what a dumb question his boss asked and boasted that not only could he boil water but that he had also boiled chicken and duck and whatever. When someone reported this to his boss, putting the kettle on every morning for the boss was added to his chores.

It happened that on the first day of his extra job, Somdet took the soot-blackened kettle down to the stream and polished it with sand until it gleamed like new. This so pleased his boss he got an old shirt and pair of jeans as a present. His being close to the boss led to further promotion as a helper in the sick bay. The workers would fall sick in turns, one or two at a time. Dispensing medicines was one of the jobs of the pick-up truck driver. Usually medical care consisted of handing out pills and having the man lie down and cover up. Shots were given occasionally and once in a long while a saline drip was administered into an arm. Being around the patients gave Somdet the chance to help dispense pills and hand this and that to the doctor until finally he became so adept at it some workers began calling him doctor too.

On that morning, Somdet squatted quietly by the fire until the kettle boiled, then, while walking around the rise over to the big camp house, his thoughts turned again to the radio and the disappearance of his friends. He intended to tell his boss what had happened, but when he got there he realized his boss already knew as he was hastily giving orders for everything to be loaded into the truck. The workers piled in the power saws and other things until it was fully loaded. When his boss turned and saw him standing like a stick with the kettle in his hand, he shouted at him, "Hey you, Somdet, you stay here. Don't forget to boil up some rice for the sick guys. I'll send the truck back for you and the others before noon. If those pests show up before the truck comes, point out to where the bags of rice are kept. If they want anything else, give it to them."

While giving his lengthy instructions, he was casting his eyes around the camp, which by then was pretty empty. Somdet was surprised his boss did not ask about his missing pals but noted he was at least kind enough to be concerned about the two sick men who had recently arrived in the infirmary.

When the commotion of people and the roar of the big truck died away, a variety of forest birds began to puff up and sing in company with the sound of the wind in the treetops.

A dispirited Somdet walked back over to the cooking hearth and prepared to make some rice gruel. As he poured the rice into the pot, his thoughts turned back to his friends and the radio and then to the reports of the fighting. "Well, if they're coming, so let them come," he muttered as he recalled some old impressions that had stuck in his mind. He visualized the time he met up with such pests before in their rumpled clothes, waving their guns at him yapping some gibberish. But when he smiled at them, they smiled back and when they saw he did not understand their language, they knocked him on the head once or twice with a gun barrel. If he met up with them again, so what? At most he'd get knocked on the head again, maybe harder than before, but he believed they would not shoot somebody who gave them a smile.

However, things turned out better than the boss foresaw. Not long after the big truck carrying all the remaining stuff had gone, and before the new patients had received even half of the saline drip administered by the boss's driver, an empty truck appeared with some workers in it. Without delay, they helped load up whatever was left. The driver yelled at Somdet and the two sick guys to hurry and collect their things. Relying on his previous experience as an assistant, Somdet slowly drew the needles from the arms of the sick people, removed the rubber tubes from the bottles, stuffed the lot into his black canvas bag and sat down to keep his patients company until they were called. The two fellows leaned on his shoulders as he helped them climb into the truck.

It was past midday and the rainy season sky was beginning to churn. Somdet thought that if the rain held off, the truck could make it up the mountain and through the pass, and get back to home ground before dark. But their luck was not so good. A little way out of the camp, it poured. While he had hoped to get through the pass before dark, by the time they made it back to the sawmill on the outskirts of town, the sun had already been down and had gone halfway up the sky again. He drew his outstanding pay and said goodbye to his sick pals who had to rest up at the sawmill barracks. He shouldered his black bag, sauntered across the morning fresh-food market, by now practically deserted, stopped at a roadside stand to pick up some sticky rice and a scrawny grilled chicken, and stood out there eating. Before long, the motorized cart from his village passed by.

Beyond the town, the road led down into the plain. The rain that fell throughout the night had washed the sky clean. The depressions and holes rutting the road were brimming with water. The long reach of road ahead looked like a paddy field prepared for seeding. On either side of the road, the broad fields were rippling with greenery, deserted.

The weather had become unpredictable and the way of planting rice had consequently changed. Farmers reaching working age put down their hoes, dropped their plows, and headed for the factories, awaiting, in their distant places, news of the weather. When the news came that the paddy fields were soaked enough for planting, they'd take leave of their employers, and hire tractors from the town or from better-off neighbors to do the plowing. They would plow in the morning, broadcast the seed in the afternoon, finishing half the rice-growing season in a day. If the rain did right by them, they would go back again to visit the fields when the ears of rice were yellow on the stalks. But a lot of them never went back.

In more recent years, the method changed: the farming was contracted out. Instructions about plowing, seeding, the variety of seed to use, harvesting, up to the final hauling of the rice into the granary were transmitted from the factories or from faraway overseas. Day by day, the estrangement of the farmer and his fields increased.

In the midday stillness, the racket of the motorized cart resounded through the village. When the cart stopped in front of his house, Somdet, dressed in his baggy blackish jeans and long-sleeved shirt with metal buttons, got out and stood watching the cart disappear for a moment before sleepily climbing up the steps into his house. He was puzzled. No one was in. Peering into the kitchen, he saw the small earthen pot of fermented fish condiment standing on the fire stand. It was still warm, which told him his mother was not far off. He set his black canvas bag down on the porch, walked over to the end of the open veranda, and dipped out a drink of water from the water jar. The cool air of the rainy season blew from across the fields against his face. The need to sleep hit him hard. He walked back under the shade of the overhanging roof and eased himself down flat on the floor next to his bag.

Still drowsy, he awoke when a voice drifted faintly into his ear. "Son, you have to go right away." The young man turned over. He showed no sign of getting up. His mother patted him lightly, then shook him until he opened his eyes.

"Son, you have to go. You have to hurry. Uncle's been on the way out already since yesterday." His mother kept at him in a long monologue. When she saw he was making no move, she added, "Your uncle has been waiting for you." While this was her invention, it was based on a gnawing likelihood since over the past two days she heard her neighbors already making their peace with the dying man.

"What are you talking about, Ma?"

The question mumbled by her son told her that he was still numb with sleep.

"I tell you your uncle's been on the way out for two days now."

136

Somdet slowly got himself upright and looked around. It was already dusk. When she saw the bewilderment on his face, his mother realized the phrase she had been using was from the old days, no longer much used. So she added, "Uncle's jaw is locked; he hasn't been able to open his mouth for two days. Everyone thought he was going to pass away yesterday. They're saying that because not all the folks have gone to him yet, some worry is holding him back. They've been getting everyone to go to him since this morning. Everybody's been. They've all assured him the debts he still owes them are forgiven. The old monk from the temple has been to see him too." Her emotions getting the better of her, his mother kept at him.

Because her senior relative was motionless the whole night as if dead but not dead, she, like everyone else in the village, thought the old man must have some unfinished business on his mind. Wanting to do him a good turn and let him go in peace, they all turned Samaritan. It was an older woman, she did not remember who, who was the first to utter the good words. "Look here, Old Kham," she said firmly, "forget about the fifty baht you still owe me for those painkillers. There's nothing owing between us now."

His mother recalled vaguely that right after that there was a quiet spell and then others spoke up but more softly. "You know, Uncle, the hundred baht I laid out for you as your share of the money we put together to buy up the fish in the temple pond last dry season, well, I forgive you that right now in this life."

"We're even on that Jasmine seed rice you owe me for from three years ago. Don't you worry. Go in peace. Just dwell on the Lord Buddha."

"Older Brother, you can have the money I gave you to pay off the interest on the Farm Bank loan. May you go to that better place."

The old lady could not recall who spoke up after that because there was a general hubbub, as though they were racing against the moment when the old fellow would take his last breath. So the names of her neighbors that the mother recited while Somdet was only half-awake became jumbled, especially since some of them, when they had forgiven one debt, later recalled a second and a third. Whether the declaration was loud or faint depended on the size of the debt. Measly debts were declared softly, big ones in a resounding voice.

"Hey, Ma, does that mean Uncle owed the whole village?" Somdet finally asked, still looking sleepy.

"Well, the only people who know if that is so are them who are speaking up because your uncle himself is on the way out. Look here, son, you have got to go and right away too." When she saw him still reluctant and starting to waver like he was going to lie down again, she yanked him up by his arm.

"Come on, now. Your uncle's most probably waiting for you to come. All the others have made their peace with him, even the old monk from the temple." In reality, the mother was just saying this. The monk did not go voluntarily. In the fervor to relieve the sick man of worldly cares, whoever thought of someone who should participate, would go and look for him. His mother thought of the monk, so took it on herself to fetch him, but got scolded so the whole temple could hear.

"You think I'm a rich Chinese money-lender that I should go and forgive Uncle Kham his debts?"

She replied ingenuously that she did not think that. "Uncle was a poor man. Maybe he's worried he doesn't have any money to pay for the prayers to be said over him when he's led to the pyre. I just want him to be at peace, real soon," his mother said.

The monk got mad at that and muttered that the villagers must think he is some kind of vulture living off the dead. "Look here, Uncle Kham was my friend. How could you think I wouldn't chant for him or conduct his body to the cremation?" he replied.

Somdet's mother said the old monk turned around and retreated into his room, but not long after, he did come, holding his old yellow robe around himself, plodding over the soft ground, backside swaying, following her into the village.

Somdet was nonplussed for a moment and then remarked plaintively, "But Ma, Uncle didn't owe me anything. I owed him."

The eyebrows on his mother's plain, flat face, resembling the surface of a small drum, came together in a frown as though she could not believe him. When he saw her stay stock still, Somdet continued. "Do you remember the rosewood stump in Uncle's paddy field; it took us a month to dig it up? We got hundreds for it. I went into town to collect the money but blew it all gambling on a TV boxing match. So I owe it to him."

Somdet was talking about the time when a trader from the city went around buying up old tree stumps left buried in the fields out of which to make furniture. It was because he got hired to do the digging and transporting to the trucks that Somdet, who in the eyes of his fellow villagers was a young fool and, at a time when anyone could get a job, was looked down on as a ne'er-do-well, got to know the logging-truck drivers. And this led to his being offered a job deep in the jungle on the far side of the mountains.

"Son, now you must go."

"But Ma, you said they go to forgive Uncle's debts."

"Well, that's why."

"You give me that 'that's why' all the time. I told you I'm the one who's in debt."

"That's why. You go tell him. He may be on the way out but you talk right into his ear."

Impressed by the amount of money her son owed, his mother reiterated what she said, "You tell your uncle in a loud voice, just like the others who were well-wishing him on up to heaven, that you're going to do a ceremony to send up to him whatever it is you owe him—that is, whenever you make that much. You hear?"

Somdet was still not cooperating. "Really, son," she persisted. "You better go. I tell you that this is, this is, umm, *intercourse.*" His mother faltered, unsure about trying out this fancy word which she had been hearing for some time now.[2]

It was already getting dark when Somdet, dressed like a town boy, climbed the steps. The five or six folks gathered around were paying attention to the sick man, so when Somdet crossed the open veranda and ducked under the eaves of the overhanging roof, no one noticed. He sat down quietly gazing at the body blanketed with a thin *phakhaoma*, hardly believing it was his uncle. The cheeks were sunken, the eyes hollow. Strands of white eyebrow were stuck against the forehead resembling the wisps of gray kapok that had been placed under his nose to show whether he was still breathing. If Somdet did not see the very arm that helped him pry up the tree stump the previous dry season, he would not have been able to say that this still frame was his old relative. Somdet gazed at that arm for a long time and then suddenly recalled the black canvas bag he carried out of the jungle.

Silently, Somdet went back down the stairs, hurried over to his house, and soon came back. Kneeling down beside the sick

2. The name of this story in Thai is *Praweni*. In Thai, the literary words *praweni*, now come to mean "sexual intercourse," and *prapheni* meaning "custom" are both derived from the same Pali-Sanskrit word. Mother, hoping the high falutin' word will do the trick, has got them muddled. While it is impossible to translate the pun, at least "intercourse" having the two meanings sexual and social, gives an air of *double entendre*.

man, without hesitation, he raised the old man's head with his left hand and rested it on his thigh. He turned and unscrewed the cap on the bottle he brought with him out of the jungle in his black bag and set it down by his side. Then with his right hand he pressed on the old man's cheeks and with his thumb forced open the mouth and began pouring the contents down the man's throat.

Recovering their wits, the astounded folks sitting around set up a high-pitched hullabaloo. But Somdet, unfazed, coolly kept pouring the liquid into the still, unresisting body until it spilled out over his uncle's face and down on to the floor.

He carefully eased the head of skin and bone back down onto the pillow and wiped his hands on his pants. The body responded with a choking sound; Uncle Kham was no longer on the way out.

Somdet got up slowly, looked around at the old people gathered there, confident in the skill that he had acquired while across the border. He puffed out his chest and muttered in a deep voice something that sounded like an incantation. "If you can inject it, you can drink it. It's bound to work."

Without speaking to anyone, he went down the steps and returned home with his head held high.[3]

1996

---

3. Observe that the villagers are chagrined and embarrassed because, with old Uncle back to life, they have unnecessarily given up their right to get paid, and those who exaggerated the amounts owed in order to gain face will become the laughing stock of the village all because of Somdet, who showed them up.

Translator's Postscript

KHAMSING'S original collection of short stories *Fa Bo Kan* in Thai, published under the pseudonym Lao Khamhawm, on which his fame is based, was first published in 1958 and was reprinted for the thirteenth time in the year 2000 by Amarin Printing and Publishing PLC. Twelve of the stories from that volume first appeared in English under the title *The Politician and Other Stories* translated by Domnern Garden and published by Oxford University Press, in the Oxford in Asia Modern Authors series in 1973, and reprinted by OUP in a revised edition in 1991.

Two of the stories newly included in this collection, *Paradise Preserved* and *I Lost My Teeth* were originally translated by Prof. Herbert P. Phillips for inclusion in his work *Modern Thai Literature* published by the University of Hawaii Press in 1987. Prof. Phillips taught anthropology at the University of California, Berkeley, until his recent retirement. The research project which Prof. Phillips refers to in his introduction provided the basis for his book *Thai Peasant Personality* published by the University of Chicago Press.

Intercourse was first published in Thai and English in 1996 by Amarin Printing and Publishing PLC, the translation by Domnern Garden.

The remaining two stories newly included, *Happy Birthday,*

Grandpa and *The Buffalo with the Red Horns,* were translated by Domnern Garden for this edition.

The collaboration of Sumalee Viravaidhya in the translation of *Sales Reps of the Underworld* and the editorial work of Michael Smithies on the first Oxford edition of *The Politician* is acknowledged with continuing thanks. All footnotes in the text are the translators'.

Over the past forty years, in some of the editions put out by a number of publishing houses, Khamsing's original texts have been "spruced up" by well-intentioned editors. The Thai text in the original Khwian Thong edition of 1958 is authentic, as is the text of *Intercourse* appearing in the Amarin publication of 2000. These were used for the translations of the first twelve stories and the final story appearing in this collection. *The Buffalo with the Red Horns* was translated from Khamsing's manuscript. In the other stories, I have relied on the best early texts available, checking with Khamsing in cases of doubt.

In my original translations, the proper names used in the stories were transliterated to give a reasonable English phonetic equivalent of the pronunciation in Thai. In this edition, the standard Royal Institute system of transcription has been used.

Domnern Garden